The Making of a
MILLINER
HAT-MAKING PROJECTS

JENNY PFANENSTIEL

DOVER PUBLICATIONS, INC.
MINEOLA, NEW YORK

Dedication

This book is dedicated to my husband, the love of my life, Bart Pfanenstiel; my parents, Linda and Ron Gerst; my sister, Heather Delaney; my mother-in-law, Judy Pfanenstiel; and all of my hat friends whose love and support has guided me through my millinery journey. My mother says it best, "You have to BELIEVE," and believe I did.

Author/Book Design: Jenny Pfanenstiel

Editor: Fielden Willmott

Proofreader: Dr. Heather Delaney

Illustrator: David Green, aka Starvin-Artist

Photographer: Steve Squall

Additional Photo Retouching: Jessica Budnick and Hayley Hall

Makeup Artist/Hair Stylist: Isidro Valencia

Still Life Stylist: Megan Wilde

Model: Cassandra Mastropaolo

Bibliographical Note

The Making of a Milliner: Hat-Making Projects, is a new work, first published by Dover Publications, Inc., in 2015.

International Standard Book Number

ISBN-13: 978-0-486-79347-4
ISBN-10: 0-486-79347-8

Manufactured in the United States by RR Donnelley
79347801   2015
www.doverpublications.com

Table of Contents

Foreword

There is power in wearing a hat.

Just ask the women who lead the entertainment and fashion industries today. Take, for example, the near obsessive media coverage of the fascinators worn by Pippa and Kate Middleton. Or the hats made famous by the legendary Isabella Blow. And, of course, Lady Gaga.

For the rest of us—say, anyone who has ever worn a couture hat by Jenny Pfanenstiel—I think Julie from Arlington Heights, Illinois, puts it best. She posted this comment on formemillinery.com:

> I purchased your hat at Arlington Million. At 67 years old I have been invisible for a number of years. That hat was like magic. Men stopped and turned to look at me. They opened doors for me. I had at least 20 men and women tell me they loved my hat. We went to a restaurant after the race and the owner came to our table and said, "you make my restaurant look good." It was a wonderful day. I got so much attention and had more fun, all because of your hat.

For years, Jenny has been drawing legions of admirers who are in awe of her millinery talent, and to those who have met her or have donned any of her stellar creations, the circumstances as to how I met Jenny might come as quite a surprise.

We met on a muggy day in May of 2009. I was an editor at *Country Living Magazine*, which was hosting an event called "Pitch Your Product," held on Chicago's lakefront. During this *Shark Tank*-like showdown, hopeful entrepreneurs were given three minutes to sell their ideas to a panel of judges: me and two enterprising women with well-established businesses they'd founded on their own.

A clearly nervous but elegantly be-hatted Jenny regaled us with her exotic designs and lifelong dreams to start a millinery shop. Her passion was obvious, her verve so clear, we briefly fell silent. Unusually so. I imagine the rest of the contestants probably hoped we'd stop critiquing or interrupting with advice.

I remember, as Jenny presented her case, that I felt honored she would consider our opinions at all. We unanimously felt that she possessed great talents—and that her business plan was sound.

Since that day, I have watched her career skyrocket from one high point to another as her creations have appeared everywhere from the pages of *Vogue, Tattler,* and numerous other magazines, to the crowns of some very distinguished heads, including Oprah Winfrey, Barbara Corcoran and First Lady Michelle Obama. All this within five years of founding her business!

Despite her overnight success, Jenny takes a very honest look at her craft in her new book *The Making of a Milliner*. She even admits she never sketches a hat pattern: "I just can't draw."

It just might be her own lack of drawing ability that makes *The Making of a Milliner* so accessible. In a breezy, conversational tone, Jenny provides thorough, step-by-step directions for nine hat designs. Her words are helpful for novices and experienced milliners alike. After reading this book, I can't help but dream about buying a wooden bowl—any size, mind you!—some sizing liquid, a few yards of parasisal, and starting to block my own original beauty.

Jenny's book is an excellent gift for the craft enthusiast. It is loaded with all sorts of hat trivia and anecdotes. Even if you never make a hat, it's a fascinating journey that allows you to become fluent in the process, tools, and materials. Once-antiquated items such as parasisal and horsehair are introduced with detailed descriptions of their special attributes. I loved discovering that the interior hatband (sweatband) is made with Petersham, a fabric often confused with grosgrain but with fluted edges so it can be shaped inside a hat.

Jenny also introduces two exciting new materials: the bamboo-based jinsin and Plastic Fantastic, both of which greatly expand the horizon of possibilities in hat making. It's worth noting that the resurgence of millinery has spurred such innovations.

From the easier hat blocking guides to the expert levels of working with jinsin, Jenny walks us through every step with an ease and confidence that will set you on your own hat-making journey.

In the end, her book is empowering and powerful—much like wearing a hat.

NATALIE WARADY

Introduction

Would you like to try on a hat? Don't mind if I do! Pull up a chair, pour yourself some tea and come along with me on this journey. Learn how to make exceptional headwear, and you may find yourself crafting incredible headpieces ranging from "everyday wear" to "runway ready." I take great pride in the craft of millinery, and I want to share with you the rich history of millinery and the skills needed to create your own beautiful hats. The art of millinery dates back centuries. My goal is to keep this craft alive, because let's be honest, who doesn't love an amazing hat!

A seemingly easy wardrobe accoutrement often becomes a conversation starter, creating the perfect statement and setting the stage for yet another memorable life moment. When I think about some of the most important events in my life, I often connect these memories with the hat that adorned my head that day. Hats not only complete your style; they create a wearable journal of life's adventures. Throughout this book, you will find a little bit of everything—from how to properly wear a hat, to the different types of hat blocks used for blocking and creating a variety of unique head pieces, to a series of exciting and fun millinery projects to get you started or to advance you through your own hat-making journey. For years, I have been teaching hat-making workshops in my studio to men and women of varying skill levels. Much like the hat-making workshops, this book is designed to increase your knowledge of hat making whether you are a beginner or an advanced milliner. No prior millinery experience is necessary.

Each hat project is laid out step-by-step for easy learning and follow-through. Like anything else, once you learn the basics and the foundation of hat making, you can experiment with the techniques to create your very own unique *chapeau*. Within each hat project, there is a list of materials needed, as well as where you can purchase them. Though I will be demonstrating a particular technique using a particular type of material, these techniques are interchangeable across different mediums, so I encourage you to play, experiment, and let your hands do the walking—don't be afraid to try new things and get creative! There are projects that include the art of blocking straw and wool over hat blocks, which provide a specific structure for the hat, while other projects call for sculpting and manipulating materials using only your hands. I am a firm believer in letting the material be your guide to a finished product. I do not sketch my hat ideas (for the simple fact that I cannot draw), but I do start from a concept created from my dreams. I really enjoy creating a hat by holding the material in my hands and twisting and turning it until it moves in a direction that is free flowing and not forced.

Practice makes perfect, and the craft of millinery is both challenging and incredibly rewarding. If your stitches are not exactly perfect or consistent, or the shape of your hat has inadvertent waves in it, this is part of your own hat-making journey, and these skills, I promise, will come with time. The key to remember is that a hat is an expression of you. It is a way to express your personality. You will often hear me say that while we may wear our hearts on our sleeves, we wear our personalities on our heads! It is with this thought, that I challenge you to see where your personality takes you.

I appreciate your interest in millinery, and I am grateful to share my passion for hat making with you. A great hat can change not only your day; it can change your life. Thank you for embarking on this journey with me.

JENNY PFANENSTIEL

What is a Milliner?

Milliner (mil-uh-ner) n.
A person who makes and sells women's hats.

The word "milliner" has a rich history and has changed over the decades. It originated in the sixteenth century and came from merchants who came from Milan, Italy, to England to sell goods such as textile fabrics, lace, gloves, straw, and ribbon. The English often referred to these merchants as Milaner, denoting the place where they came from, but was pronounced "mil-uh-ner." Eventually the name stuck, and the spelling changed to "milliner."

In the 1800s and 1900s, a milliner became known as a shop owner who made and sold specialty clothing and hats from imported fabrics. Customers would often go to a milliner to buy clothing for the whole family, who were looking to stay on the cutting-edge of fashion trends. Today, a milliner is a person who has mastered the art of hat making. It is a highly respected profession in which the skilled milliner creates handmade hats from scratch using the age-old tradition and techniques of blocking material over hat blocks. Many of these blocks are very old and reflect styles of the period in history in which a hat became popular. Milliners often make custom hats for a specific clientele by working closely with their clients; measuring their heads, choosing specific materials

and creating special hats just for them. A milliner today must incorporate a fashion-forward blend of raw talent, imagination, and modern technology.

The making of hats is a craft I have come to admire, respect, and for which I have a true passion. I take great pride in capturing the time-honored traditions in my work; however, I am also an experimenter. I love working with a material (perhaps even in a nontraditional way) and coming up with new ways in which to create something. Through the knowledge that I have gained over the years, I have been able to take what I have learned and make it my own through my interpretations of what I have found works best in making hats through trial and error as a modern day milliner. It is the drive to succeed and the ability to weather the ups and downs of a specialty business that has carried most modern American milliners to where they are today. Milliners come together with one common thread, and that is the love of hat making and the desire to continue a tradition that is by no means forgotten.

I encourage you, too, to create hats and make them your own. Through these hat projects from this book and others, you will be on your way to "The Making of a Milliner".

How to Measure Your Head

Measuring Head with Tape Measure

In order to purchase the right hat, you must know your own head measurement. If you go to a milliner to have a custom hat made, they will measure your head for you. To measure your own head, get a tape measure and locate the bump on the back of your head. Some bumps are more pronounced than others. Place the tape measure underneath the bump and wrap it above your ears and finish approximately one inch above your eyebrows. The tape measure should fit comfortably as you would like your hat to fit. The average size head is 22.5", but this can vary depending on how much or how little hair you have. If you change your hairstyle often, this may affect the fit of your hat.

Now that you know your head size, you know the size "crown" to use with the following projects. If you plan to make a hat for someone else, you will need to know their head size and use that size crown accordingly.

Choosing a Hat

A hat is a wonderful and fashionable accessory. It should be a reflection of you as a person. There is no right or wrong time to wear a hat. If you feel like wearing a hat to the grocery store or to the opera, let your personality shine through your hat.

Yes, everyone can wear a hat! It is simply a matter of finding the shape that best suits your face shape and hairstyle. The position of a hat on the head should be adjusted for the most flattering effect. A hat can look completely different when worn on the back of the head than if worn on the front of the head with a slight tilt to the side. Just that little tweak can make a world of a

difference. I always recommend a slight tilt to every hat.

Most importantly, you want to choose a hat that fits appropriately. If it is too small, you will probably end up with a headache; too big, and it will slip over your eyes. A hat should fit comfortably with no pain or discomfort.

I have included some face shapes below. Find the shape that best matches yours. I have listed some of the more popular hat shapes and the face shapes that tend to work best with each. However, I do recommend experimenting with different shapes, to determine which hat shape works best for you.

Face Shapes

ROUND

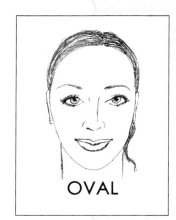
OVAL

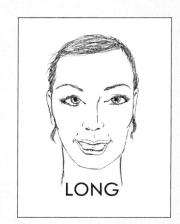
LONG

TRIANGLE

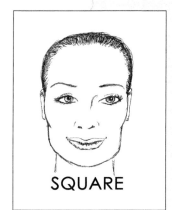
SQUARE

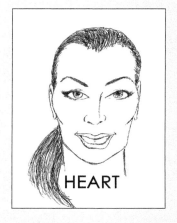
HEART

HAT SHAPES

Large Brim. A traditional shape for the horse races and useful in summer to block the sun. This hat looks great on a longer face shape, such as the heart, oval, and triangle. This hat also looks great on people with longer hair and who have some height.

Flipped-Up Brim. This hat is a good choice for someone who wants a large brim hat, but may get swallowed under it. This hat looks great on round and square face shapes. It also suits people with shorter hair because the hat allows the hair to show more on the one side.

Fedora. Most face shapes and hair lengths can wear this hat. Fedoras can come in various brim widths, but most are flat and stick straight out in the front or have a very slight bend, so the brim doesn't cover the face. Worn with a slight tilt, this hat is a superb everyday look.

Fascinator. This hat is a dramatic look for most face shapes and hair lengths. If you are looking to add height to your appearance, this is a great choice. The fascinator is the perfect statement piece for any event.

Cloche. A classic piece. The cloche brim can come in many variations. It can face straight down as shown, or it can flip up in the front and/or back. The brim can be designed and worn so that this hat can look great on anyone. A brim facing straight down looks great on faces that are more oval or triangle-shaped, with hair that is a bit longer. Brims that are flipped up in the front look great on round or square faces and with long or short hair. A longer face such as a heart or oval looks best when the brim is flipped up in the back.

Face and Hat Shapes created by Illustrator: David Green, aka Starvin-Artist

LARGE BRIM

FLIPPED UP BRIM

FEDORA

FASCINATOR

CLOCHE

Hat Blocks

Hat Block (blok) n.
A mold or form in which wood has been carved into a shape
of a hat for the purpose of molding material to make a hat.

Antique wooden hat blocks can be hard to find. Many were burned in World War II by people trying to keep warm in the cold winters. In addition, milliners burned their hat blocks after each season, so others would not be able to copy their work. Since the decline of millinery in the United States, there are fewer hat block makers, but you can still find master block makers overseas who have been creating beautiful wooden blocks for decades.

Though most hat blocks are made of different types of wood, you will also find them made with aluminum, styrofoam, or polyurethane. In the different projects that follow, you will work with styles of blocks that can be purchased at block-making supply houses throughout the world. If you don't have the exact hat block that is called for in the instructions, you can apply the same technique to most shapes. If you do not want to invest in hat blocks right away, common materials found in your own kitchen such as bowls, saucers, and plates, can also be used. Some of the projects use a wooden bowl, so you can see how this process works. Your local thrift store can also be a good place to search for inexpensive bowls or other appropriate items to use.

When investing in your first hat block, it is best to start with a simple shape. Once you have measured your head, you will know the correct size crown to purchase. The next common block to purchase is a brim. They are oval and can come in a solid piece of wood, or with a hole in the center.

Blocks can be carved right side up or upside down. A hat block that is made right side up, clearly shows what the final hat will look like. However, with an upside down block, you have to flip the image in your mind to picture what the final hat will look like.

Not every hat uses separate crown and brim blocks. Some use a "one block," which consists of a brim and crown in one piece. Some just use crowns, like the pillbox, or most cloche blocks. The Plastic Fantastic Cloche on page 35 is an example of a hat that uses a cloche block with the crown and brim together.

Wool and straw have different requirements when blocking them. Each material requires different pressure to be used when stretching and manipulating it. Pull too hard and you can create a hole, pull too little and bubbles or waves can occur in the finished product. They are two different animals, and you will eventually learn the possibilities and limitations of both. This is why I encourage you to use the projects in this book to create hats from both straw and wool.

Crowns

BLOCK TYPES

Crown Block. The part of the hat that covers the head. It is important to know the head size of the person who will be wearing the hat, in order to choose the appropriate size crown. Here are some examples of different crown shapes:

Low Dome; short crown

High Dome; tall crown

Pill; flat crown

Fedora; crown with an indentation in the middle

Brims

Brim Block. The brim is the part of the hat that extends outward from the crown.

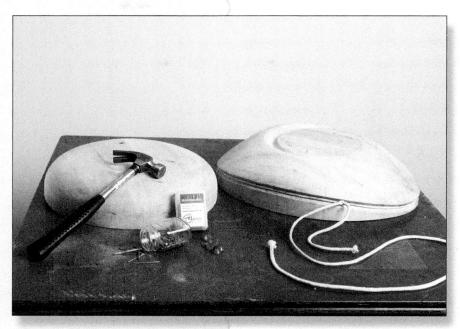

Brims With and Without Rope Lines

Rope Lines vs. No Rope Lines. A rope line is a groove that has been made in the brim block for a rope to sit in to help keep the material stretched and in place. Any rope $\frac{1}{4}$-inch thick or less that fits in the groove, including common clothesline, can be used. When using blocks that do not have rope lines, nail or tack down the material to hold it in place and keep its shape during the blocking and drying process. Millinery tacks can be purchased for this purpose. Thin nails that measure at least 2 inches long can also be used.

To use a rope line, first measure how much rope you will need. Wrap the rope around the area where you will use it. Add an extra 5 to 8 inches of rope and cut it. Next, make a slipknot in the rope. This will allow you to easily tighten and loosen the rope as you use it. If you were ever in Girl or Boy Scouts, you learned this knot. To make a slipknot, take both ends of the rope (tails) and face them upwards. Take one of the ends and tie a loose knot ending with the tail facing up. Now, slide the other tail through the loose knot, so both tails are facing up. Tighten the knot around the loop, and you have a slip-knot. Pull the unknotted tail to tighten the loop and pull on the loop to make it larger. This is how you will be using this rope when blocking.

One Blocks

One Blocks. The crown and brim are combined in a single block and used together to make a hat.

Cloche Block; a block used to make a style of hat that became popular in the 1920s.

Upside Down Block; an inverted hat that is created literally upside down.

Fascinator / Cocktail Blocks

Fascinator/Cocktail Block. This block is typically small. It can come in many different shapes including circles, ovals, cones, hearts, and mini top hats. The fascinator sits on top of the head rather than covering the head like a hat. It is held on with a headband, elastic, or comb.

Disk Block. Disk blocks can come small or large. Commonly used as a block to make a fascinator or hatinator—a fascinator and hat in one—it sits on your head like a fascinator, but it's large like a hat.

Most disk blocks are upside down or inverted blocks, which means you are making the hat upside down, opposed to right side up.

Disk Blocks

Puzzle Block. This block consists of multiple pieces (typically five) that create the shape of the hat. This allows the hat maker to easily remove the material from the block without ruining the blocked shape. The puzzle block is flipped upside down and pieces are removed until the blocked material slides off easily.

Puzzle blocks are rare and expensive. If you come across one, I highly recommend buying it. It can even make a great showpiece on your mantel.

Puzzle Block

Kitchen Block. A wooden bowl found in your kitchen. Examples can include small salad bowls, or saucers.

Kitchen Blocks

Hat Stand or Block Spinner. A hat stand is used to prop up a crown block when working on it. Most crown hat blocks have three holes on the bottom of them. The two holes on each end are used to hold the block with your fingers in order to remove the blocked material. The hole in the middle is used to place the block on a hat stand when blocking, so you can reach underneath the hat. It is also used to spin the hat around when working on different angles of the hat without having to pick it up and turn it. Hat stands are also used during the drying process in order to prop up the crown, so air can get under the block.

Hat Stand / Block Spinner

Dummy Head. A wooden or canvas head that is primarily used when sculpting a hat by hand. The material can be pinned into the canvas of the dummy head to keep it in place when working with it.

Dummy Heads

Protecting Your Block. Before using your hat block, cover it to protect it from water, dyes from the materials, and other damage that can result from wear and tear. Depending on what the hat block is made of, changes in temperature and humidity can affect it. It can be covered with tinfoil and plastic bags. I have found that Glad® brand Press'n Seal® plastic wrap works best, and I use it on all my hat blocks. When laying the plastic wrap over the hat block, don't worry about it being completely smooth. Small pleats and folds won't interfere in the blocking process.

Block Protection

Millinery Materials

Wool Materials

WOOL

Wool can be purchased in many colors and finishes and can also come in different faux prints. Wool can also be dyed using boiling water, and either acid or natural dyes.

There are many different types of wool. In the millinery industry, we use millinery grade 100% wool; a nonwoven material with compressed fibers. It can be combined with rabbit and beaver fur strands, or velour fibers.

Wool for hat making comes in different forms, called hoods and capelines. These are pieces that have been roughly molded by the manufacturer as a starting point for the milliner. Hoods are small cone shapes, which are used for smaller hats such as crowns, pillboxes, and cloches. The capeline is essentially a larger hood that has a brim. This is used for bigger hats that include a crown and brim together. Another option is flat felt wool. This comes flat like fabric and is sold by the yard or meter. Flat felt is commonly used for wool sculpted hats, pattern hats, or blocked hats where you want to block only the brim and not the crown with it.

STRAW

Sinamay. Sinamay is made from banana plant fibers and has a more open weave than parasisal and other straws. Sinamay can come in different weaves including crocheted, basket, knotted, cobweb, mesh, and more. It comes in many different colors and prints and can also be dyed.

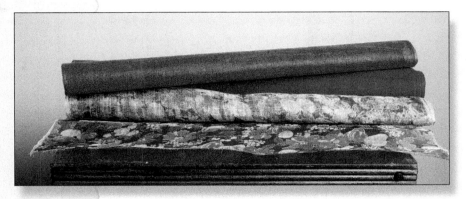

Sinamay

Sinamay is bought by the yard or meter, just like fabric. It can sometimes be found as a hood or capeline, but most sinamay is made flat. It is best used to create larger brims, or disk-block shaped hats. Sinamay is also a great material for free form sculpting, allowing you to explore new hat shapes and embellishments by manipulating the sinamay with your hands.

Parasisal. Parasisal is a fine, high quality, natural straw that is woven from the fibers of the sisal plant. Typically a very tight weave depending on the grade of the parasisal, it is also easily dyed.

Parasisal is available in the form of hoods or capelines. Just like wool hoods or capelines, the hoods are best used for various crowns, small cloche blocks, and hats without brims like pillboxes. Parasisal capelines are best used when blocking a crown and brim together. Parasisal can also be used to hand sculpt hats into beautiful shapes.

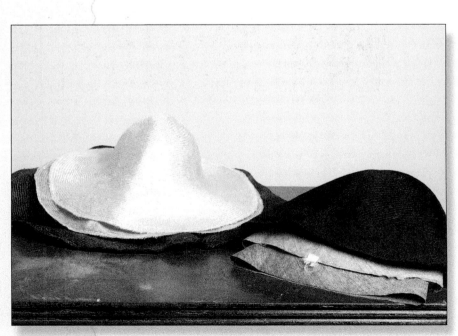

Parasisal

HORSEHAIR OR CRINOLINE

Horsehair, also called crinoline, is a synthetic material commonly used to make fascinators. You do not block horsehair, but instead sculpt it to create beautiful embellishments; it can also be used for the edge of a brim, or veiling.

Horsehair is a fun and versatile material to work with because it can be manipulated in many ways to create a variety of effects like bubbles; and the ends can be frayed, or tied off to create a smooth finish. The possibilities with horsehair are endless.

Plain Horsehair

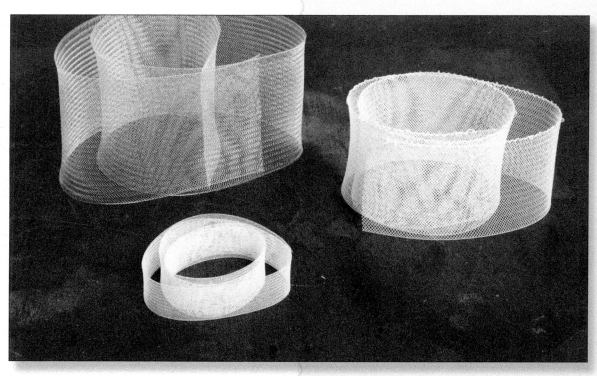

Stiffened Horsehair

Horsehair comes in many widths from ¹/₂" wide to 8". It can be flat or tubular. It comes plain, in color or clear, and stiffened or non-stiffened, and decorative with beauty marks (small dots throughout the horsehair), pleated, striped, tubular, and printed with leopard spots or other patterns.

Decorative Horsehair

Pleated Horsehair

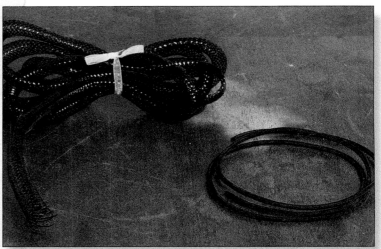

Tubular Horsehair

VEILING

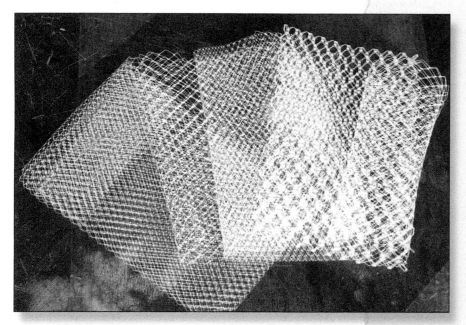

Veiling

Veiling is traditionally used for bridal headpieces. It can fall behind the head covering the hair, also called a train, and be very long. A birdcage veil can lie gently in front of the face covering just the eyes, or it can fall over the entire face. Veiling comes in different decorative patterns. The veilings shown are examples of Russian veiling, honeycomb veiling, diamond veiling, and merry widow veiling with and without pearls.

Veiling is sold by the yard and comes in 9" and 18" widths.

JINSIN

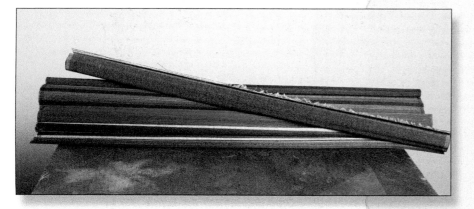

Jinsin

Commercially known as a form of bamboo, jinsin is actually made from the leaf stalks of the buri palm or fan palm.

Jinsin comes in two widths—36 inch, which is the most common, and 45 inch. It is sold by the yard or meter.

It comes in great colors and patterns, from vibrant solids to creative stripes. Jinsin can also be dyed, and since it is made of a natural fiber, it picks up the dyes easily. Sculpting with jinsin is similar to basket weaving in that the fiber needs to be saturated as you work to keep the fibers from breaking.

Jinsin is a versatile material that can be sculpted into beautiful bows, turbans, circles, and loops.

PLASTIC FANTASTIC

Plastic Fantastic is thermoplastic material that is moldable under heat, using hot water and steam, or a heat source such as a heat gun or hair dryer. It comes in a stiff polymer sheet, and once it is heat activated, it can expand to three times its original size when pulled from all directions. You may need an extra pair of hands when stretching the Plastic Fantastic depending on how big you are planning on stretching it.

Plastic Fantastic

MILLINERY WIRE

Most of the projects in this book use millinery wire to provide structure to the brims. Millinery wire can also be used to shape embellishments.

Millinery wire comes in black or white and in different gauges. Wire comes in gauge widths from 16 to 24. The lower the gauge, the bigger the wire width. Some milliners prefer to use very thin wire (larger number), so they can shape the wire themselves. I prefer to use a thicker wire (smaller number) because I want the wire to hold its shape, especially when used to provide structure to a brim. The projects in this book call for 18–21 gauge millinery wire.

Millinery Wire and Joiners

Millinery wire eventually needs to be joined inside the hat. This can be accomplished a couple of different ways. The ends of the wire can be overlapped and sewn together, or wire joiners can be used to hold the ends together. In my experience, joiners hold better and also keep the width the same around the whole wire. Overlapping the wire to sew it doubles the width in that place.

Joiners are placed on the ends of the wire to create a continuous circle all the way around and fastened using pliers.

PETERSHAM

Petersham is used for the "sweat-band" inside the hat, which provides comfort where the hat meets the head. Petersham is often confused with grosgrain. However, Petersham has a scalloped edge, which allows it to be curved easily with an iron. Use Petersham with a fiber content of at least 50% cotton for the best results. Grosgrain has a smooth edge and does not lie flat when it is curved.

Petersham comes in different widths. The projects in this book call for a $7/8$" width. Use pinking shears to cut the Petersham and prevent the ends from fraying.

Petersham

ELASTIC

Elastic is commonly used to hold on fascinators or cocktail hats. You can purchase it in precut lengths with metal edges for easy insertion, or you can buy elastic by the yard and cut it yourself. Precut elastic comes in white or black, but it can be dyed to match your hair color.

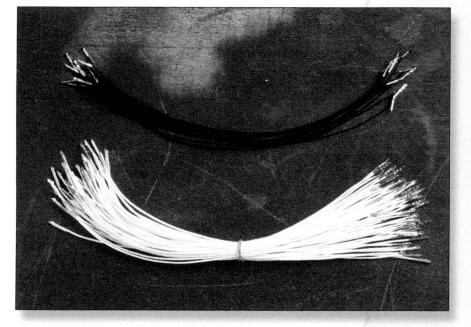

Elastic

Straw and Wool Sizing

SIZING

Sizing is used to stiffen the blocked material. Different sizing is used for straw or wool. Both can be purchased from millinery suppliers, and the directions for using them are on the containers. The sizing is applied at different times in the process, depending on whether straw or wool is being treated.

Straw. Straw sizing is sprayed on the outside of the straw once it is blocked and secured just before setting the hat aside for drying.

Wool. The wool is first saturated and steamed prior to adding the sizing. The sizing is sprayed on the inside or wrong side of the wool just before blocking.

Hatpin Stems

HATPINS

The stem of a hatpin typically measures four to eight inches long. One end of the hatpin is the pinhead, a flat piece of metal which will keep any beads or other embellishments from slipping off. The other end of the hatpin is the point. It is sharp so the wearer can stab it through the material of the hat. Today, most hatpin points are protected with an end piece that slips over the point so the wearer does not injure themself or others.

Hatpins are primarily used to hold your hat to your head by going through your hair. They can also be used on lapels and bags as decorative pieces.

A hatpin can be created with beads, brooches, earrings, flowers, buttons, or anything that strikes your fancy.

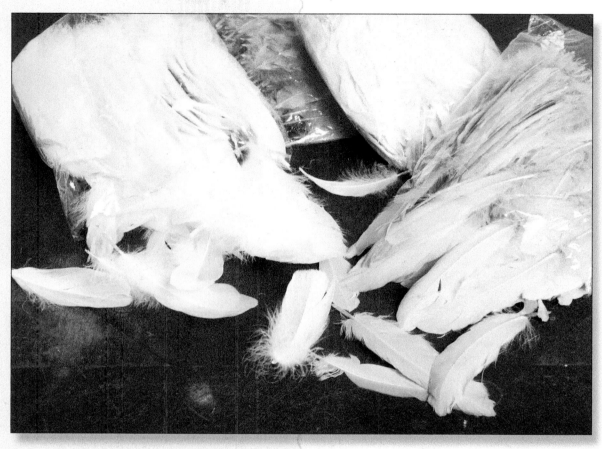

Feathers

FEATHERS

Feathers come in all shapes, sizes, and colors. Feathers can be dyed and are easy to shape with scissors and your hands. The type of food that the bird eats often causes the natural colors of the feathers. For instance, flamingos are actually born with white feathers, but turn pink from the algae and small animals that they eat. Feathers have had many uses throughout the decades.

Making your own feather flowers is a wonderful craft. It can be very pleasing to place each feather to create a unique embellishment. Commercial feather flowers can be very expensive to purchase, so crafting your own is a useful skill.

The Feather Flower project (page 113) in this book, will teach you the basics of flower making.

Hats

Hat (hat) n.
A shaped covering for the head.

A hat can be worn for protection against the elements, for ceremonial purposes, religious reasons, or as a fashion accessory. In the past, hats were an indicator of social status, especially in the southern United States. In the 1800s, women preferred not to tan, so they wore bigger hats to keep the sun off their faces. In those days, people assumed that anyone with a tan worked in the fields, which suggested a lower social class.

In the early 1900s, it did not matter if you were poor or rich, young or old, man or woman; you never left the house without a hat. In fact, most etiquette books discussed how disgraceful and disrespectful to others it would be if you left the house with your head uncovered.

The 1960s changed many fashion traditions, including hairstyles. When bigger hairstyles became more popular, hats were discarded. This was a factor in the eventual decline of the millinery industry.

Today, functional hats are still being worn for occupations, religious purposes, and to protect oneself from the weather. Others simply wear hats as a fashion statement and appreciate the sophistication and elegance a hat can provide. A hat is an excellent addition to any wardrobe, casual or dressy; it will be the first thing a person will notice about you, and will always be a timeless accessory.

Wool Cowboy Hat

The cowboy hat is a perfect everyday hat and a good go-to for that bad hair day, or just a great accessory with jeans and a T-shirt or a skirt and blouse. This style can be made casual or dressy by simply changing the embellishments. The cowboy hat shape can also be made in straw for those hot summer days when you are looking for a hat to protect you from the sun.

This project uses an antique upside down, or inverted, cowboy hat block. The crown and brim will be used as a one block. This hat is blocked while looking at the inside of the hat. The crown fits down inside the brim block. All upside down one blocks work in this way, so if you are working with a different shaped upside-down block, the steps may not be similar.

Tools and Materials

WHERE TO BUY:

Wool capeline –
  Judith M Millinery

Millinery wire and joiners –
  Judith M Millinery

Petersham – Jolie Femmes

Upside down cowboy
  block
Wool capeline
Plastic wrap (Press'n Seal
  recommended)
Water bin
Squirt bottle
Hot Water
Towel
Wool sizing
Steamer
Rope for brim
Thread to match wool
Needle
Approximately 2 yards of $^7/_8$"-wide
  Petersham

Pins
18 to 21 gauge millinery wire
Wire joiner
Pliers
Wire cutters
Iron
Scissors
Sewing machine
Superglue gel
Pinking sheers
Weights (bags of sand or rice
  can be used)
Feathers
Button

Prepare. Cover the hat block with plastic wrap to protect it from steam, water, and any dyes.

Get your steamer ready to go, and have rope, weights, and wool sizing in your squirt bottle at hand.

Covering the Hat Block

Soak. Fill the water bin with enough hot water to cover the material when submerged. Soak the wool in the hot water. Move the fabric around in the water bin as it soaks to ensure all parts of the wool are saturated.

Let it soak for approximately 15 minutes.

Soaking causes the wool fibers to relax and open up. As the wool dries over the block, the fibers close to maintain the shape in which it has been formed.

Soaking the Wool

Spraying Sizing on Wool

Stretch. Turn on the steamer. Remove the wool from the bin and gently squeeze out the excess water. Do not wring out the water. Gently squeeze the wool.

Now spray the sizing into the inside of the wool, making sure to spray the entire inside, reaching the center and all edges. Rub the wool back and forth in your hands to massage the sizing into the wool. Once that is completed, lay the wool over the hat block.

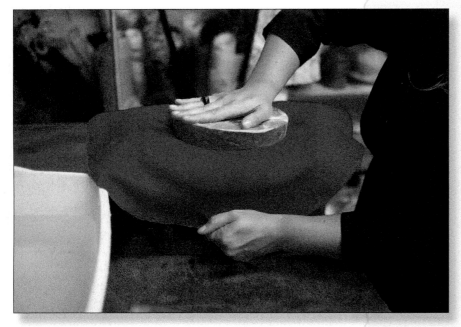

Blocking Wool

Because this is an upside down hat block, it has a crown mold that will go inside the brim block during the blocking process. Stretch the wool over the hat block in all directions. Set the crown mold in its place. Press down on the crown block, and steam the wool in each section. Continue to pull the wool on all sides to ensure any pleats, wrinkles, bumps, and bubbles are removed. It may also be helpful to place a weight or sandbag on top of the crown to help push it down. Repeat this process as needed until the wool is stretched and completely smoothed out. It can take practice to know how much you need to pull on the material in order to make it perfectly smooth. Continue to use the steam throughout the stretching process to keep the wool fibers loose.

Secure. Make a slipknot in the rope (see page 7), and place the loop over the block so that the wool is between the rope line and the rope. Tighten the slipknot. Stretch the wool a few more times while tightening the rope as you go. Once you feel that the wool is tight, secure, and with all pleats and wrinkles removed, add the weight to the crown. Put it aside to dry completely. Wool takes at least 24 hours to dry. It helps to put a fan on it and rotate the block throughout the day.

Wool Roped Down

Cut. Once the blocked wool is completely dry, it is ready to be trimmed before it is removed from the block. Before removing the rope, cut the excess wool all the way around approximately 1 inch from the rope line. The wire will eventually sit in and be sewn to the rope line, and the excess wool will be trimmed again. The edge does not need to be perfect at this time.

Remove the rope and the crown mold from the brim. Carefully remove the blocked wool from the block. Turn the hat right side up to reveal the shape of a cowboy hat.

Blocked Wool with Cut Edge

29

Breaking the Back of the Wire

Wire. Wiring a hat is optional if the material is stiff enough or if you want a floppy brim. For this hat, we will be using 18–21 gauge millinery wire.

First, measure how much wire you will need. Wrap the wire around the outside of the brim, add 3", and cut with wire cutters. Because most wire is wound up when you buy it, it helps to take some of the curve out. I call this breaking the back of the wire. Slide your thumb along the curve of the wire from top to bottom. You are not trying to re-bend it or straighten it, just trying to take a little bit of the curve out.

Next, we are going to add the wire joiner to one of the ends of the wire. Millinery wire is covered with two main threads that can be easily removed by grabbing one of the threads and pulling it away from the wire. Remove the thread exposing $1/2$" of the wire. Do the same with the second thread. Cut the loose thread off. Dab a very small amount of superglue gel onto the tip of the exposed wire. Then, place half of the wire joiner onto the wire. The other half will be used later to join the other end of the wire. Take your pliers and squeeze the half of the joiner that is over the wire to clamp it closed.

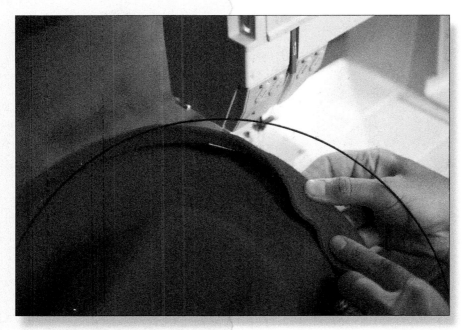

Sewing Wire into the Wool Brim

Sew. Your sewing machine should have the same color of thread as your wool. We will be sewing a straight stitch at a 3.5 stitch length.

Place the wire in the fold of the brim. Begin sewing at the center back of the hat with the end of the wire with the joiner about 2" above the starting point so it is easy to access the joiner later on, in order to join the other end of the wire.

Keep the wire in the fold as close to the edge as possible. Sew as close as possible to the wire without breaking a needle. For beginners, I suggest starting ½" from the edge and, if comfortable, sewing at ¼" from the edge. Cradle the hat in one hand as you sew. Sew the wire around the whole hat, stopping 4"–5" before the end. Measure the remaining wire to the center of the joiner and cut. Once the wire is cut, remove the thread from the wire, exposing ½" of wire. Place a small dab of superglue gel on the end of the wire and place it inside the joiner and squeeze down with the pliers to close. Finish sewing the wire into the hat, ending with a backstitch.

Trim the excess wool along the brim as close as possible to the sewn line you just made. Next, smooth out the cut wool edge by running your scissor blade back and forth over the edge of the brim to fluff the wool up. This is done so it doesn't look so much like a cut edge. If you plan to cover the edge with trim, you can omit this step.

Completed Sweatband

Sweatband. Measure the Petersham around the inside of the hat where the crown meets the brim. Begin at the center back and pin every 2" around the hat. Be sure not to pull or stretch the Petersham as you pin, because this can cause your wool to tighten or loosen and will result in your crown becoming smaller or bigger. Pin the Petersham gently all around, and cut it with pinking shears to avoid fraying, leaving an extra inch at the end to be folded over for a finished look.

Start with a single strand of thread that matches the color of the wool. You will be making little stitches that will show on the outside of the hat, which will be covered later by the crown band. Working along the edge of the Petersham where the crown meets the brim, hand sew a straight stitch all around using stitches that are 1/4" long and that bump up to each other on the inside. If your stitches are too long or too far apart, the Petersham will have gaps. Our goal is for it to lie nice and smooth against the hat. The Petersham is left open at the top edge so it has room to expand when you put your head inside. Remove the pins as you go, and finish by knotting the thread.

Fun Facts

The cowboy hat is also referred to as a ten-gallon hat. There are many theories as to how this phrase came about. One theory is that the term ten-gallon is a corruption of the Spanish modifier *tan galán*, which loosely translates as "really handsome."

Completed Crown Band

Crown Band. Turn your iron to the cotton setting. Put the hat on the crown block to hold it in place and to ensure you are measuring the outside band to the exact measurement of the crown block. Wrap the Petersham around the outside of the crown where it meets the brim. Add about 1" to 1 ¹/₂" so you can fold it over nicely for a finished look.

We use the iron to create a nice curve in the Petersham. Because Petersham has scalloped edges, it will lie flat against the crown of the hat when it is sewn on. Start at one end and begin to iron, shaping the curve with your other hand as you go. When finished, you should have a curved band.

Take the curved band and place it around the crown where it meets the brim, with the bigger edge of the curve closest to the brim. Put the ends of the Petersham where your embellishment will go so they will be hidden under the embellishment. The embellishment should not be placed directly center front, or to the side, but in between those points. To keep the band in place, tack down the bottom edge (closest to the brim) by hand. You want to tack down every 3" to 4" all the way around. Be sure not to sew through the sweatband on the inside of the hat. Keep your stitches underneath the sweatband.

Embellish. Group together some coordinating feathers and sew around the ends so they stay together. Place the group of feathers behind the crown band and tack it down. To complete the embellishment, sew a button over the band where the feathers meet.

You have just completed your hand-blocked wool cowboy hat.

Plastic Fantastic Cloche

The classic cloche is made modern by adding a new and unique material to the crown. Try this project with and without the Plastic Fantastic to create two different cloche looks.

This is a two-part technique. First the cloche is blocked. When it is completely dry, the embellishment, which is the Plastic Fantastic, is added.

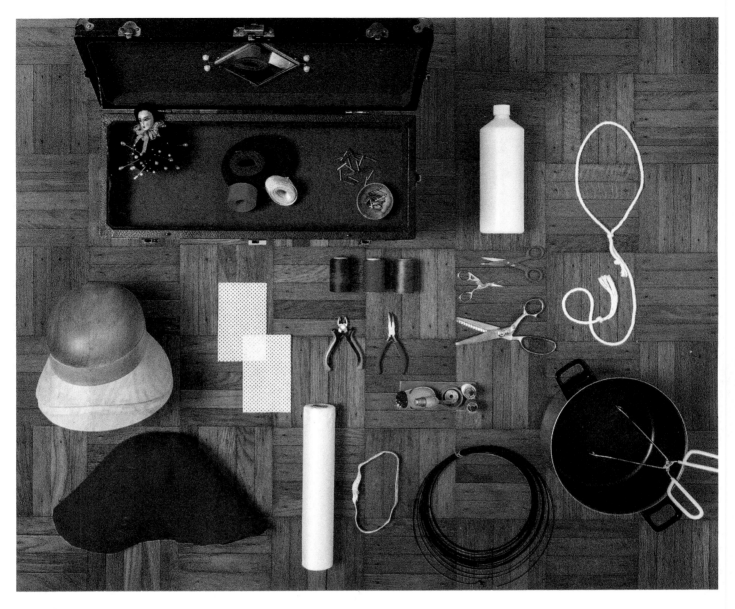

WHERE TO BUY:

Cloche hat block –
  Guy Morse-Brown

Plastic Fantastic –
  Torb & Reiner

Wool hood –
  Judith M Millinery

Millinery wire and joiners –
  Judith M Millinery

Petersham – Jolie Femmes

Tools and Materials

Cloche hat block	Steamer
One sheet of Plastic Fantastic	Scissors
Wool hood	Pins
Boiling water	Thread to match wool
Water bin	Tongs
Pot	Needle
Towel	Pinking shears
Elastic for crown	2 yards of $7/8$" Petersham
Rope for brim	18–21 gauge millinery wire
Plastic wrap (Press'n Seal recommended)	Wire joiners
Squirt bottle for sizing	Wire cutter
Wool sizing	Pliers
Iron	Superglue gel
	Embellishments

PART 1—CLOCHE

Prepare. Cover the hat block with plastic wrap to protect it from steam, water, and any dyes.

This cloche block is a one block, which means the crown and brim are together, and the cloche is blocked as one piece. It is also right side up, so the material is blocked with the right side out.

Many cloches can look the same from the front and back, so it is important that you mark it to keep track as you work.

Get your steamer ready to go, and have rope, and wool sizing in your squirt bottle at hand.

Covering Hat Block

Soak. Fill the water bin with enough hot water to cover the material when submerged. Soak the wool in the hot water. Move the wool around in the water bin as it soaks to ensure all parts of the wool are saturated. The wool should begin to feel softer and looser. Let it soak for approximately 15 minutes.

Soaking causes the wool fibers to relax and open up. As the wool dries over the block, the fibers close to maintain the shape in which it has been formed.

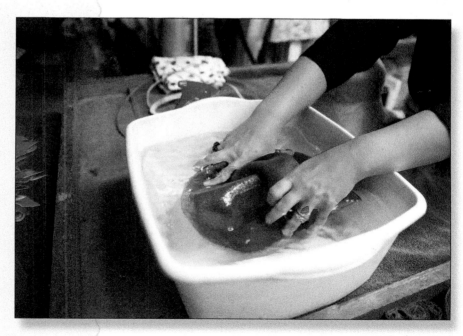

Soaking Wool

Spraying Sizing on Wool

Stretch. Turn your steamer on. Remove the wool from the bin and gently squeeze out the excess water. Do not wring the water out. Gently squeeze the wool.

Now, spray the sizing into the inside of the wool, making sure to spray the entire inside, reaching the center and all edges. Then, rub the wool back and forth in your hands to massage the sizing into the wool. Once that is completed, place the wool over the hat block.

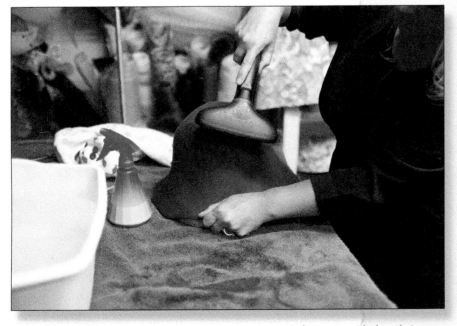

Stretching Wool Over Hat Block with Steamer

Stretch the wool over the hat block in all directions. This is where your steamer comes in handy. As you work with the wool, use the steamer in the areas where you are pulling to keep the fibers loose, allowing you to continue to stretch it. Your goal is to get all of the pleats, wrinkles, bumps, and bubbles out so the wool is completely smooth.

Blocked Wool with Elastic and Rope

Secure. Make a slipknot in the rope (see page 7) and place the loop over the block so that the wool is between the rope line and the rope. Use the steamer to stretch the wool a few more times while tightening the rope as you go. Once you feel that the wool is tight and secure with all of the pleats and wrinkles removed, place the elastic around the crown where it meets the brim. This will ensure the fit at the crown. Set the blocked wool aside to dry completely. Wool takes at least 24 hours to dry. It helps to put a fan on it and rotate the block throughout the day.

Cut. Once the blocked wool is completely dry, it is ready to be trimmed before it is removed from the block. Remove the elastic from the crown. Before removing the rope at the brim, cut the excess wool all the way around approximately 1" from the rope line. This does not have to be perfect because once the wire is sewn in the excess wool will be cut away more precisely.

Carefully remove the blocked wool from the block.

Breaking the Back of the Wire

Wire. Wiring a hat is optional if the material is stiff enough or if you want a floppy brim. For this hat, we will be using 18–21 gauge millinery wire.

First, we need to measure how much wire we will need. Wrap the wire around the outside of the brim, add 3", and cut with wire cutters. Because most wire is wound up when you buy it, it helps to take some of the curve out. I call this breaking the back of the wire. Slide your thumb along the curve of the wire from top to bottom. You are not trying to re-bend it or straighten it, just trying to take a little bit of the curve out.

Next, we are going to add the wire joiner to one of the ends of the wire. Millinery wire is covered with two main threads that can be easily removed by grabbing one of the threads and pulling it away from the wire. Remove the thread exposing $1/2$" of the wire. Do the same with the second thread. Cut the loose thread off. Dab a very small amount of superglue gel onto the tip of the exposed wire. Then, place half of the wire joiner onto the wire. The other half will be used later to join the other end of the wire. Take your pliers and squeeze the half of the joiner that is over the wire to clamp it closed.

Securing Wire Joiner

Sew. Your sewing machine should have the same color of thread as your wool. We will be sewing a straight stitch at a 3.5 stitch length.

Place the wire in the fold of the brim. Begin sewing at center back of the hat with the end of the wire with the joiner about 2" above the starting point so it is easy to access the joiner later in order to join the other end of the wire.

Keep the wire in the fold as close to the edge as possible. Sew as close as possible to the wire without breaking the needle. For beginners, I suggest starting $1/2$" from the edge and, if comfortable, sewing at $1/4$" from the edge. Cradle the hat in one hand as you sew. Sew the wire around the whole hat, stopping 4"–5" before the end. Measure the remaining wire to the center of the joiner and cut. Once the wire is cut, remove the thread from the wire, exposing $1/2$" of wire. Place a small dab of superglue gel on the end of the wire and place it inside the joiner and squeeze down with the pliers to close. Finish sewing the wire into the hat, ending with a backstitch.

Trim the excess wool along the brim as close as possible to the sewn line you just made. Next, smooth out the cut wool edge by running your scissor blade back and forth over the edge of the brim to fluff the wool up. This is done so it doesn't look so much like a cut edge. If you plan to cover the edge with trim, you can omit this step.

Completed Sweatband

Sweatband. Measure the Petersham around the inside of the hat where the crown meets the brim. Begin at the center back and pin every 2" around the hat. Be sure not to pull or stretch the Petersham as you pin, because this can cause your Petersham to tighten or loosen and will result in your crown becoming smaller or bigger. Pin the Petersham gently all around, and cut it with pinking shears to avoid fraying, leaving an extra inch at the end to be folded over for a finished look.

Start with a single strand of thread that matches the color of the wool. As you sew, you will be making little stitches that will show on the outside of the hat, which will be covered later by the crown band. Work-ing along the edge of the Petersham where the crown meets the brim, hand-sew a straight stitch all around using stitches that are $1/4$"-long and that bump up to each other on the inside. If your stitches are too long or too far apart, the Petersham will have gaps. Our goal is to have it lie nice and smooth against the hat. The Petersham is left open at the top edge so it has room to expand when you put your head inside. Remove the pins as you go, and finish by knotting the thread

Place the cloche back on the block and set it aside. Next, we will be preparing the Plastic Fantastic and will need the cloche on the hat block nearby.

Soaking Plastic in Boiling Water

PART 2—PLASTIC FANTASTIC

Prepare. Boil a pot of water. Turn on your steamer and grab your rope, tongs, a towel, and an extra pair of hands (enlist a friend or spouse if available). If you do not have an extra pair of hands, no problem, your steamer will help you through these next couple of steps.

Removing Plastic with Tongs

Soak. Place the Plastic Fantastic in the boiling water. After a minute it will become translucent. If it doesn't, your water is too cold, and you need to start over. Once the plastic starts to turn clear, move the plastic around gently in the water with the tongs to ensure that all parts of the plastic become translucent.

Stretching the Plastic by Hand

Stretch. Get your cloche ready to go because you will be stretching the Plastic Fantastic over the cloche crown. The plastic will stretch to three times its original size, creating a unique finished look with the wool peeking through the plastic holes. Work quickly, because the plastic dries really fast, so you want to stretch it over the crown and secure it with rope where it meets the brim as quickly as possible.

It may take a couple of tries to get the hang of it. If you make a mistake, just put the plastic back into the boiling water and start over. The plastic will shrink back to its original size as long as the water is hot enough.

When you pull the plastic out of the water with the tongs, you and your friend want to stand on opposite sides of the hat and pull the plastic over the crown of the cloche by the edges. Don't worry if you go past the point where the crown meets the brim because you will cut away any excess plastic once it is dry.

If there are areas where the plastic doesn't get stretched enough before it dries, use your steamer on that section, and stretch it with your hands to the desired length.

Once you have the plastic where you want it, rope it down. Let the Plastic Fantastic dry completely—about ten minutes. Once dry, use scissors to cut away any excess plastic that went past where the crown meets the brim. A crown band will be added to cover the raw edge of the plastic. The excess plastic can be used to make an embellishment later.

Tack the plastic to the wool crown where the crown meets the brim every 3"–4" inches. Avoid sewing through the sweatband. Keep the stitches underneath it.

Completed Crown Band

Crown Band. Turn your iron to the cotton setting. With your hat sitting on the block, take the Petersham and wrap it around the crown where it meets the brim, making sure it is covering the raw edge of the plastic. Add 1"–1¹/₂" so the end can be folded over nicely for a finished look.

We use the iron to create a nice curve in the Petersham. Because Petersham has scalloped edges, it will lie flat against the crown of the hat when it is sewn on. Start at one end, and begin to iron, shaping the curve with your other hand as you go. When finished, you should have a curved band.

Take the curved band and place it around the crown where it meets the brim, with the bigger edge of the curve closest to the brim. Put the ends of the Petersham where your embellishment will go, so they will be hidden under the embellishment. The embellishment should not be placed directly center front, or to the side, but in between those points. To keep the band in place, tack down the bottom edge (closest to the brim) by hand. You want to tack down every 3" to 4" all the way around. Be sure not to sew through the sweatband on the inside of the hat. Keep your stitches underneath the sweatband.

Embellish. The sample is embellished with a coordinating Petersham band, but feel free to add a button or flower.

You have just completed your hand-blocked cloche hat with a Plastic Fantastic crown. Amazing!

Fun Facts

Cloche is the French word for "bell." This hat was made famous in the 1920s by the flappers. It has been said that the fashion icon Coco Chanel created the first cloche hat.

Straw Brim Hat

The straw brim hat is perfect for those sunny days at the beach, or to compliment your new sundress. Embellish this hat with feathers and flowers, and you are ready for the horse races! This hat is very versatile and works for most occasions.

The crown and brim for this project are made separately and sewn together. Be sure to choose a crown block that is the correct head size. See "How to Measure your Head" on page 1.

Tools and Materials

Crown block
Brim block
Parasisal hood
2 yards of sinamay
Plastic wrap (Press'n Seal
   recommended)
Water bin
Hot water
Towel
Straw sizing
Squirt bottle
Steamer
Rope for brim
Elastic for crown
Hammer
Nails or millinery tacks

Tailor's chalk
Thread to match the crown
   and brim
Needle
2 yards of $7/8$" Petersham
Iron
Pins
18–21 gauge millinery wire
Wire joiner
Pliers
Wire cutters
Superglue gel
Sewing machine
Scissors
Pinking sheers
Buttons

PART 1—BRIM

Prepare. Cover the crown and brim blocks with plastic wrap to protect them from steam, water, and any dyes. Set the crown block aside.

Get your steamer ready to go, and have rope, and straw sizing in your squirt bottle at hand.

Measure out the amount of sinamay that you will be using on your brim block. Two layers of sinamay are used for this hat. This is the norm in the industry. Two layers are used to provide strength and durability to the hat. One layer would not be sturdy enough.

Lay your roll of sinamay over the brim hat block so that there are 2" of excess sinamay all around. Cut. Repeat for the second layer.

Soak. Fill the water bin with enough hot water to cover two layers of sinamay when submerged.

Soak both layers of straw in the hot water. Move the straw around in the water bin as it soaks to ensure all parts of the straw become saturated. Soak for 10 to 15 minutes.

Stretch. Turn your steamer on. Take one layer of straw out of the water and let it drip dry. Place it over the brim block and smooth it out with your hands. Then, take the second layer of straw out of the water, let it drip dry, and lay it cross-grained over the first layer. Smooth it out with your hands

Soaking Sinamay

Laying Straw Cross-Grained Over Brim Block

49

Spraying Sizing on Straw

Secure. Make a slipknot in the rope (see page 7) and place the loop in the rope line along the edge of the brim block so that the straw is between the block and the rope. Once secure, gently stretch the straw starting with the bottom layer to get all of the pleats and bumps out of it. Do this all around the hat block. Once you have completed the bottom layer, repeat this process with the top layer. Tighten the rope as you stretch the straw to be sure it stays secure. Use your steamer as needed to keep the fibers moist and pliable. Once you think you have gotten all of the pleats and bumps out, take your hand and slide it all over the straw. If you feel a bump, that section needs more stretching. Look at the straw from all directions; be sure both straw layers are touching and that there are no gaps. This process can take a lot of practice. Straw is very different from wool, and it will show every pleat and bump if not perfectly smoothed out. If the straw is not secured with enough tension, it will shrink during the drying process, creating un-wanted waves. It is very important to take your time with each step.

Sizing. Now that your straw is completely stretched, it is time to apply the sizing. Take your squirt bottle and spray the straw sizing over the blocked brim straw. Be sure to spray all areas, including the edges where the rope lies.

Once everything looks great, let it dry over-night. It helps to put on a fan and turn the block periodically.

PART 2—CROWN

Prepare. Have your elastic, nails or tacks, and hammer ready to go. The crown has no rope line, so you will be nailing the straw in place directly to the block.

Soak. Fill the water bin with enough hot water to cover the parasisal when it is submerged. Use clean water so that the run-off dyes from the sinamay don't affect the parasisal.

Move the straw around in the water bin periodically to ensure all parts of the straw are saturated. Soak for 10 to 15 minutes.

Stretch. On the top of a parasisal straw hood, there is an "X" or box shape where the beginning of the straw was woven; this is the center. When stretching the parasisal over your crown, be sure to center that shape on top of the crown block.

Remove the straw from the water and let it drip dry. Place it over the crown block and smooth with your hands. Place the elastic over the crown near the base. Make sure the top of the parasisal is centered, and continue to stretch and smooth out the straw until all pleats and bumps are removed.

Secure. Flip the crown block over. Since the crown does not have a rope line, you will be nailing the straw to the block to secure it. It is important to nail in all four directions of the crown first, and then work in between. I refer to this as nailing at the north, south, east, and west points. Always nail in this manner because it is easy to pull the straw off center without realizing it.

Sizing. Once the crown is stretched on the block, spray it with straw sizing. Make sure you spray all over the crown, including the edges. Let it dry overnight.

Crown Secured with Nails and Elastic

Cutting Excess Straw from Crown Along Edge

PART 3—CROWN AND BRIM

Cut. Once both blocked pieces are completely dry, they are ready to be trimmed. Let's start with the brim. Before removing the rope, cut the excess straw all the way around approximately 1" from the rope line. This does not need to be perfect because when the wire is sewn in later, the excess straw will be cut away more precisely. Find the center back and center front of the brim and place a pin in each to mark it. Put the brim aside for a moment to work on the crown.

Find the center back and center front of the crown. Mark with pins. Remove the elastic and nails from the crown. Cut away the excess straw at the edge of the bottom of the crown. It is important that this is trimmed perfectly, not too long, and not too short, but exactly at the edge. The edge of this crown is going to sit on top of the brim and will eventually be sewn to the brim.

Place the crown on top of the brim. Center the crown, matching up the center front and center back pins. If your brim is a perfect circle, then measure your crown so it is even all around. The sample uses an oval crown that is wider on one side. This brim also has an indentation where the crown goes, so that is where I am placing it. Once the crown is in place, trace the outline of your crown onto the brim straw with tailor's chalk. Remove the crown and set it aside. You should now have an oval-shaped chalk mark where your crown will eventually be sewn in place.

Cut Tabs on Brim

Take your scissors and puncture a hole through both layers of your brim straw in the center of the chalk oval. Cut a slit from the center of the oval to the chalk line. Starting from the center again, make another slit to the chalk line one inch away from the previous slit. We are creating tabs that will eventually stick up inside the crown, which we will use to hand-sew the brim to the crown. Once you have gone around the entire outline, trim each tab to 1" in height. Bend each tab back so that it stands straight up.

Remove the rope from the brim. Carefully remove the blocked straw from the brim block.

Sew the two brim layers together with a running stitch along the chalk line. This will create extra strength where the straw has been cut to ensure that the brim straws do not move while we are pinning the crown to them. Use the same color thread as the brim straw, as these stitches will not be removed.

Pin. Place the crown on the brim, matching the crown pins to the brim pins and placing the crown over the tabs that are sticking up. The crown should sit flush against the brim with no open spaces. Pin the crown to the brim tabs starting with the north, south, east, and west points, and then pinning in between. Pinning parallel to the brim works best.

Sewing Crown to Brim

Sew. Thread a needle with a double strand of thread that matches the color of the crown straw. A contrast color of thread was used for the photo so you can see my stitches. Starting at center back, take your needle and poke through the crown from the underneath to hide your thread knot (about ¼" up from the brim). Once you have come up through the crown, take your needle and go straight down into the brim where it meets the crown edge. When starting your stitch, do this a couple of times in a row to secure the beginning stitch. Go over about ¼" to ½" and repeat these steps. Come up the back side of the crown and go straight down into the brim where it meets the crown. Be sure that your thread does not get caught on the straw tabs underneath as you sew. When it has a raw edge, sinamay tends to grab sewing thread, and you don't want to be left with loops that have been caught on the straw. Remove the pins when all of the sewing is completed. These stitches will be eventually covered with the crown band.

Completed Sweatband

Sweatband. Measure the Petersham around the inside of the hat where the crown meets the brim. Begin at the center back and pin every 2" around the hat. Be sure not to pull or stretch the Petersham as you pin, because this can cause your straw to tighten or loosen and will result in your crown becoming smaller or bigger. Pin the Petersham gently all around and cut it with pinking shears, leaving an extra inch at the end to be folded over for a finished look.

Start with a single strand of thread that matches the color of the crown straw. As you sew, you are making little stitches that show on the outside of the hat, which will be covered later by the crown band. Working along the edge of the Petersham where the crown meets the brim, hand-sew a straight stitch all around using stitches that are $1/4$" long and that bump up to each other on the inside. If your stitches are too long or too far apart, the Petersham will have gaps. Our goal is for it to lie nice and smooth against the hat. The Petersham is left open at the top edge so it has room to expand when you put your head inside. Remove the pins as you go, and finish by knotting the thread.

After you have sewn in the sweatband, trim any tabs sticking out past the sweatband.

Breaking the Back of the Wire

Wire. Wiring a hat is optional if the material is stiff enough or if you want a floppy brim. For this hat, we will be using 18–21 gauge millinery wire.

First, we need to measure how much wire we will need. Wrap the wire around the outside of the brim, add 3", and cut with wire cutters. Because most wire is wound up when you buy it, it helps to take some of the curve out. I call this breaking the back of the wire. Slide your thumb along the curve of the wire from top to bottom. You are not trying to re-bend it or straighten it, just trying to take a little bit of the curve out.

Next, we are going to add the wire joiner to one of the ends of the wire. Millinery wire is covered with two main threads that can be easily removed by grabbing one of the threads and pulling it away from the wire. Remove the thread exposing $1/2$" of the wire. Do the same with the second thread. Cut the loose thread off. Dab a very small amount of superglue gel onto the tip of the exposed wire. Then, place half of the wire joiner onto the wire. The other half will be used later to join the other end of the wire. Take your pliers and squeeze the half of the joiner that is over the wire to clamp it closed.

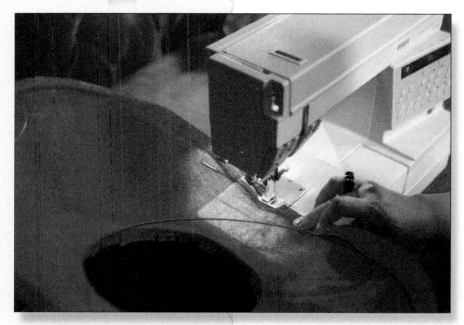

Sewing Wire into the Straw Brim

Sew. Your sewing machine should have the same color thread as the brim. We will be sewing a straight stitch at a 3.5 stitch length.

Place the wire in the fold of the brim. Begin sewing at the center back of the hat with the end of the wire with the joiner about 2" above the starting point so it is easy to access the joiner later in order to join the other end of the wire.

Keep the wire in the fold as close to the edge as possible. Sew as close as possible to the wire without breaking a needle. For beginners, I suggest starting $1/2$" from the edge and, if comfortable, sewing at $1/4$" from the edge. Cradle the hat in one hand as you sew. Sew the wire around the whole hat, stopping 4"–5" before the end. Measure the remaining wire to the center of the joiner and cut. Once the wire is cut, remove the thread from the wire, exposing $1/2$" of wire. Place a small dab of superglue gel on the end of the wire and place it inside the joiner and squeeze down with the pliers to close. Finish sewing the wire into the hat, ending with a backstitch.

Trim the excess straw, cutting it as close as possible to the line you just sewed.

Completed Trim Along Brim Edge

Trim. Turn your iron on and set it to the cotton setting. We will be using Petersham for the trim. Measure the Petersham around the edge of the brim, adding 2" so it can be folded under at the end for a nice, finished look. Cut the Petersham with pinking shears to keep it from unraveling. Fold the Petersham in half lengthwise and iron in the crease. Wrap the Petersham over the edge of the brim. As you sew the trim on, you can bump up the fold to the edge of the brim, to ensure that the Petersham lies evenly on both sides of the brim edge.

Now we are going to machine sew the ironed Petersham to the brim using a 3.5 zigzag stitch length, by 3 wide. Start at the center back using thread that matches the color of the Petersham. Sew slowly as your wire is close to the edge, and you do not want to break a needle.

When you get to about 2" from the end, fold the Petersham under, and overlap the starting point with the fold. Finish sewing over the folded end.

Fun Facts

The term "mad as a hatter" dates back to the Victorian era, and originates from hat makers who experienced prolonged exposure to mercury vapors while working with wool. In France, the practice of using mercury vapors in hat making ended in 1898 when a law was passed to protect the hat makers. In the United States, the practice continued until 1941.

Completed Crown Band

Crown Band. Turn your iron to the cotton setting. Put the hat on the crown block to hold it in place and to ensure you are measuring the outside band to the exact measurement of the crown block. Wrap the Petersham around the outside of the crown where it meets the brim. Add about 1"–1½" so you can fold it over nicely, for a finished look.

We use the iron to create a nice curve in the Petersham. Because Petersham has scalloped edges, it will lie flat against the crown of the hat when it is sewn on. Start at one end, and begin to iron, shaping the curve with your other hand as you go. When finished, you should have a curved band. Take the curved band and place it around the crown where it meets the brim, with the bigger edge of the curve closest to the brim. Put the ends of the Petersham where your embellishment will go, so they will be hidden under the embellishment.

The embellishment should not be placed directly at the center front, or to the side, but in between those points. To keep the band in place, tack down the bottom edge (closest to the brim) by hand. You want to tack down every 3" to 4" all the way around. Be sure not to sew through the sweatband on the inside of the hat. Keep your stitches underneath the sweatband.

Remove any chalk residue with your fingernail or a light brush.

Embellish. Use your imagination to embellish anyway you like. The sample is embellished with a series of mismatched black buttons, which are arranged randomly and tacked down individually.

This hat uses advanced techniques including the additional hand sewing, so you should be proud of yourself for completing it.

Fascinators

Fascinator (fas-uh-ney-ter) n.
A decorative head covering worn
on formal occasions, usually
consisting of feathers or flowers.

A fascinator can be called a cocktail hat, perch, topper, or head-piece. A fascinator sits on your head, whereas a hat covers your head. Fascinators have been extravagant eye-catchers since their origin in the seventeenth century. Women often wore ships and stuffed birds in their powdered wigs to gain attention.

Fascinators are typically one-size-fits-all and are worn with elastic to secure them to your head. The elastic is not worn uncomfortably under your chin like a birthday hat, but rather it goes under your hair and bumps up behind your ears. A fascinator should sit on your forehead at an angle about two inches or two finger widths above one of your eyebrows. Once you have the hat in position, your hair is brushed over the elastic to hide it. Elastic works better than a headband or comb to keep the hat in place while still allowing you to move your head freely.

Fascinators can be a great addition to any outfit. Whether you are going dancing, to the opera, the races, a wedding, or tea with the girls, a fascinator is always a great accessory. The next four projects will invite you to explore your creativity with traditional and non-traditional materials. Let your imagination soar. Fascinators make great sculptural headpieces. If creating with your hands is your cup of tea; you will enjoy making these hats using some fun materials.

Fascinator Disk

Are you looking to make a statement? The fascinator disk is sure to turn heads. Create an elegant headpiece that is perfect for a black tie gala or a show-stopping piece for the horse race. Make it to complement your outfit by embellishing it to match the color and style you are wearing. The sample was embellished with a black, beaded dress in mind.

This project is blocked on an upside down disk block. Instead of blocking the fascinator with the outside of the fascinator showing, you will be blocking while looking at the inside of the fascinator. The presser lies in the hole of the disk block during the drying process and creates the indentation for your head.

Tools and Materials

WHERE TO BUY:

Disk Block –
  Guy Morse-Brown

Sinamay –
  Jolie Femmes

Millinery wire and joiners –
  Judith M Millinery

Petersham – Jolie Femmes

Upside down large disk hat
  block with presser
Dummy head
2 yards of sinamay
Plastic wrap
  (Press'n Seal recommended)
Water bin
Hot water
Towel
Straw sizing
Squirt bottle for sizing
Steamer
Rope for disk edge
Sand bags for weights
Scissors

Pins
Thread to match the sinamay
Thread to match the Petersham
Needle
18–21 gauge millinery wire
Wire joiner
Pliers
Wire cutters
Superglue gel
Sewing machine
2 yards of ⁷⁄₈" Petersham
Pinking sheers
Satin headband
Beads
Flowers

Prepare. Cover the disk hat block and the presser with plastic wrap to protect them from steam, water, and any dyes. Set the presser aside.

Get your steamer ready to go, and have rope, weights, and straw sizing in your squirt bottle at hand.

Measure out the amount of sinamay that you will be using on your disk block. Two layers of sinamay are used for this fascinator. This is the norm in the industry. Two layers are used to provide strength and durability to the hat. One layer would not be sturdy enough.

Lay your roll of sinamay over the disk block so that there are 2" of excess sinamay all around. A presser is used with this block. Take into consideration that extra straw will be needed when the presser sits on the block during the drying process. It is better to have too much straw than not enough. Cut. Repeat for the second layer.

Soak. Fill the water bin with enough hot water to cover two layers of straw sinamay when submerged.

Soak both layers of straw in the hot water. Move the straw around in the water bin as it soaks to ensure all parts are saturated. Soak for 10 to 15 minutes.

Measuring Sinamay over Disk Block

Soaking Sinamay

Laying the Two Layers of Sinamay Cross-Grained

Stretch. Remember, this is an upside down disk block, so the first layer of straw that you lay down is the straw that will be exposed when you have the hat on. If you are using a print sinamay, or two different colors of straw, the first layer that you lay down is the one that will show when the hat is on.

Turn your steamer on. Once the straw is ready, take the first layer out of the water and let it drip dry. Place it over the hat block and smooth it out with your hands. Then take the second layer of straw, let it drip dry and lay it cross-grained over the first layer and smooth it out with your hands.

Secure. Make a slipknot in the rope (see page 7) and place the loop in the rope line along the edge of the disk block so that the straw is between the block and the rope. Once secure, gently stretch the straw starting with the bottom layer to get all of the pleats and bumps out of it. Do this all around the hat block. Once you have completed the bottom layer, repeat this process with the top layer. Tighten the rope as you stretch the straw to be sure it stays secure. Use your steamer as needed to keep the fibers moist and pliable. Once you think you have gotten all of the pleats and bumps out, take your hand and slide it all over the straw. If you feel a bump, that section needs more stretching. Look at the straw from all directions; be sure both straw layers are touching and that there are no gaps. This process can take a lot of practice. Straw will show every pleat and bump if it is not perfectly smoothed out. If the straw is not secured with enough tension, it will shrink during the drying process, creating unwanted waves. It is very important to take your time with each step.

Sizing. Now that your straw is completely stretched, it is time to apply the sizing. Spray the straw sizing over the blocked straw. Be sure to spray all areas including the edges where the rope lies.

Once the sizing has been sprayed, it is time to put the presser on the block. Place the presser on the straw over the opening in the block, and place a weight on the top to ensure enough pressure is being added to properly shape the hat. If the straw shifts when the presser and weight are placed, keep the presser and weight in place and adjust the straw by stretching it again in those areas. Let it dry overnight. It helps to put on a fan and turn the block periodically.

Cut. When the blocked straw is completely dry, it is ready to be trimmed. Remove the presser. Before removing the rope, cut the excess straw all the way around, approximately 1" from the rope line. This does not need to be perfect because when the wire is sewn in; the excess straw will be cut away more precisely.

Remove the rope. Carefully remove the blocked straw from the block. Slide your fingers under the straw and go gently around, releasing it from the plastic and the block. Repeat this process until the straw can be removed without misshaping the blocked straw. Take your time. Do not force it. When you turn the hat right side up, you will see the shape of the fascinator, where your head will sit, and where we will be sewing in a headband later.

Spraying Sizing on Blocked Straw

Straw Drying with Presser in Place

67

Sewing Wire in Straw Edge

Wire. We want the fascinator to stay stiff and hold its disk shape. We will be using 18–21 gauge millinery wire.

First, we need to measure how much wire we will need. Wrap the wire around the outside of the brim, add 3", and cut with wire cutters. Because most wire is wound up when you buy it, it helps to take some of the curve out. I call this breaking the back of the wire. Slide your thumb along the curve of the wire from top to bottom. You are not trying to re-bend it or straighten it, just trying to take a little bit of the curve out.

Next, we are going to add the wire joiner to one of the ends of the wire. Millinery wire is covered with two main threads that can be easily removed by grabbing one of the threads and pulling it away from the wire. Remove the thread, exposing $^1/_2$" of the wire. Do the same with the second thread. Cut the loose thread off. Dab a very small amount of superglue gel onto the tip of the exposed wire. Then, place half of the

wire joiner onto the wire. The other half will be used later to join the other end of the wire. Take your pliers and squeeze the half of the joiner that is over the wire to clamp it closed.

Sew. Your sewing machine should have the same color thread as the straw. You will be sewing a straight stitch at a 3.5 stitch length.

Before sewing the wire in, crease both layers of straw together with your fingers at the indent left by the rope, working all the way around the edge. This will help to keep the wire in the fold when sewing.

Place the blocked straw on your head, look in the mirror, and decide on which side of the head you want it to sit. Mark the center back with a pin. Begin sewing at the center back of the hat with the end of the wire with the joiner about 2" above the starting point so it is easy to access the joiner later in order to join the other end of the wire.

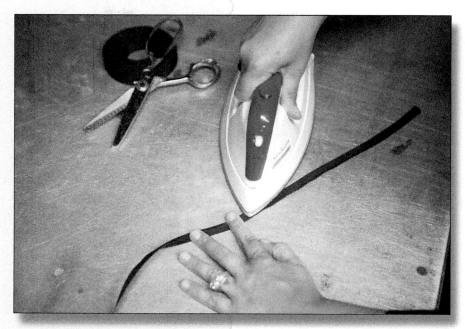

Ironing Petersham Trim in Half

Place the wire in the fold of the brim as close to the edge as possible. It is important that both layers stay together as the wire is being sewn in. Sew as close as possible to the wire without breaking a needle. For beginners, I suggest starting $1/2$" from the edge and, if comfortable, sewing at $1/4$" from the edge. Cradle the hat in one hand as you sew. Sew the wire around the whole hat, stopping 4"–5" before the end. Measure the remaining wire to the center of the joiner and cut. Once the wire is cut, remove the thread from the wire, exposing $1/2$" of wire. Place a small dab of superglue gel on the end of the wire and place it inside the joiner and squeeze down with the pliers to close. Finish sewing the wire into the hat, ending with a backstitch.

Trim the excess straw as close to the sewn line as possible without cutting into your stitches.

Trim. Turn your iron to the cotton setting. We will be using Petersham to give the edge of the brim a nice, finished look. Measure the Petersham around the edge of the brim, adding 2", so it can be folded under at the end. Cut the Petersham with pinking shears to keep it from unraveling. Fold the Petersham in half lengthwise, and iron the crease in. This way when you sew the trim on, you can bump up the ironed edge to the edge of the brim to ensure that the Petersham is lying evenly on both sides.

Sew. Next, sew the ironed Petersham over the brim using the sewing machine. Using thread that matches the color of the Petersham; use a zigzag stitch at a 3.5 stitch length. Start at the center back and go slowly because your wire is close to the edge and you don't want to break a needle.

Hand Sewing on Headband—Crossing Over the Headband on Top

Headband. This fascinator is held on with a purchased headband that is hand-sewn in. It is easy to sew into the satin of a satin headband. The headband can be found at a local craft store.

Place the headband on your head, grab your fascinator and pins, and look into the mirror. Hold the fascinator up to your head and place it where you want it to sit on your head. Once you have positioned it, pin the fascinator to the satin headband so it will not shift while you are sewing the headband in place.

Thread a needle with a double strand of thread that matches the straw. Flip your hat upside down so you are looking at the headband. Starting at the pins on one end, sew through the satin headband with stitches perpendicular to the headband. Do this three times to secure the first stitches. Then, go straight up into the straw, next to the headband, cross over to the other side of the headband, and come straight down through the straw catching the edge of the satin with your needle. Sew at an angle underneath the satin of the headband, about 1/4" from the previous section.

Hand Sewing on Headband—Sewing Through Satin Headband at an Angle.

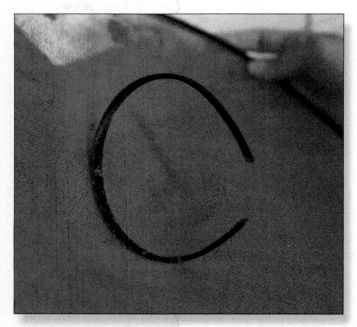

Completed Headband

Then, take your needle and go straight up into the straw again, cross over to the other side of the headband, and come straight down through the straw, catching the edge of the satin with your needle. Repeat this process until you get to the other end. Avoid sewing over your pins so you don't have loose threads when the pins are removed. Repeat this process by starting on the opposite end and going back the other way, sewing over the same stitches that you did before.

Remove pins once this is completed.

Embellish. The sample is decorated with vintage flowers and beading. Place your hat on a dummy or wig head. This way you can style on the top of the hat easily while the hat sits in place. Pin different flowers and other trims around your hat. Once you have an arrangement that you like, tack each one down with matching thread. Do not glue your embellishments on.

You have just completed your very own disk fascinator!

Fun Facts

Kate Middleton, Duchess of Cambridge and the wife of Prince William, is often seen wearing disk fascinators.

Bridal Fascinator

Are you a bride-to-be, or do you know someone who is? You can create your own memorable bridal headpiece with veiling, by following these simple steps.

For this project, you will be making a beautiful bridal hat with a birdcage veil. The block for this hat is a wooden bowl. The one used for the sample is approximately $5^{1}/_{2}$" in diameter. If you don't have a similar one in your kitchen, you can find something at your local thrift store.

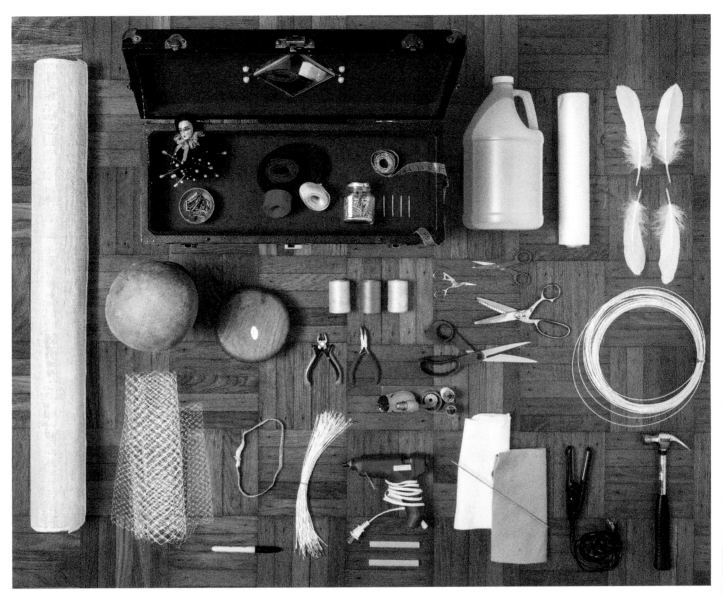

Tools and Materials

WHERE TO BUY:

Sinamay –
   Jolie Femmes

Veiling –
   Judith M Millinery

Feathers –
   Moonlight Feathers

Millinery wire and joiners –
   Judith M Millinery

Elastic – Judith M Millinery

Petersham – Jolie Femmes

Wooden kitchen bowl
Dummy head
Sinamay
20" of 9"-width Russian veiling
Measuring tape
Feathers (see "Making a Feather
   Flower" project on page 113)
Plastic wrap (Glad Press'n Seal
   recommended)
Water bin
Hot water
Towel
Straw sizing
Squirt bottle for sizing
Steamer

Elastic for crown
Hammer
Nails or millinery tacks
Scissors
Pins
Thread
Needle
18–21 gauge millinery wire
Wire joiner
Pliers
Wire cutters
Super glue gel
1 yard of 7/8" Petersham
Pinking sheers
Elastic strap for fascinator

Soaking Sinamay

PART 1—BASE

Prepare. Cover the kitchen bowl with plastic wrap to protect it from dyes and water, keeping your block in good condition for years to come. This also prevents the straw from sticking to the block.

Measure out the amount of sinamay that you will be using on your brim block. Two layers of sinamay are used for this hat. This is the norm in the industry. Two layers are used to provide strength and durability to the hat. One layer would not be sturdy enough.

Lay your roll of sinamay over the brim hat block so that there are 2" of excess sinamay all around. Cut. Repeat for the second layer.

Soak. Fill the water bin with enough hot water to cover both layers of straw when submerged.

Soak both layers of straw in the hot water. Move the straw around in the water bin as it soaks to ensure all parts of the straw are saturated. Soak for 10 to 15 minutes.

Stretch. Turn your steamer on. Take one layer of straw out of the water and let it drip dry. Place it over the hat block and smooth it out with your hands. Then, take the second layer of straw out of the water, let it drip dry, and lay it cross-grained over the first layer. Smooth it out with your hands.

Secured Straw with Nails and Elastic

Secure. Place the elastic over the straw to hold it on the bowl. Then gently stretch the straw, starting with the bottom layer to get all of the pleats and bumps out of it. Do this all around the hat block. Repeat for the top layer. The straw can begin to dry as you work with it, so use the steamer to keep the fibers loose, allowing you to continue to stretch it.

Flip the block over. Since the block does not have a rope line, the straw is nailed or tacked to the bowl to secure it as it dries. It is important to nail in all four directions of the crown first, and then work in between. I refer to this as nailing at the north, south, east, and west points. Always nail in this manner because it is easy to pull the straw off center without realizing it.

Finally, take your hand and slide it over the straw all around, if you feel a bump, that section needs adjusting. Look at the straw from all directions to be sure both straw layers are touching and there are no gaps. This can take a lot of practice. Straw will show every pleat and bump if not perfectly smoothed out. The straw must be tightly secured during the drying process or it will shrink unevenly, creating waves in the fabric. It is very important to take your time with each step.

Sizing. When the straw is completely stretched and secure, spray the straw sizing over the blocked straw. Be sure to spray all areas including the edges where it is nailed in.

Let it dry overnight. It helps to put a fan on it and turn the block periodically.

Cut. Once the blocked straw is completely dry, it is ready to be trimmed before removing it from the block. First, remove the elastic and nails. Then, cut the excess straw all the way around approximately 1" from the brim edge. This does not need to be perfect because once the wire is sewn in later, the excess straw will be cut away more precisely.

Carefully remove the blocked straw from the kitchen block. Slide your fingers under the straw and go around slowly, releasing it from the plastic and the block. Repeat this process until the straw can easily be removed without misshaping it. Do not force it.

Wire Joined at Both Ends with Joiner

Wire. In order for the fascinator to stay stiff and keep the circular shape, we will be using 18–21 gauge millinery wire.

For this project, the wire is joined at both ends before it is sewn in, so the measurement must be exact. The wire is preset and pinned in place so that the fascinator maintains the upright, circular shape. When working with a small circular shape such as this one, it is best to keep the natural curve of the wire as it comes from the coil. If we do not do the wire this way, the circle will turn into a flat plate.

Next, we are going to add a wire joiner to the end of the wire. Millinery wire is covered with two main threads, which can be easily removed by grabbing one of the threads and pulling it away from the wire. Remove the thread, exposing $1/2$" of the wire. Do the same with the second thread. Cut the loose thread off. Dab a very small amount of superglue gel onto the tip of the exposed wire. Then, place half of the wire joiner onto the wire and use the pliers to clamp it closed. Repeat this process on the other end of the wire. When completed, your joined wire should fit perfectly in the folded edge of the straw.

Sewing Wire in Straw Edge by Hand

Sew. It is difficult to machine sew the wire into a small base without deforming it. So for this project, the wire will be sewn in by hand. Use a double strand of thread that is the same color as the straw. For the purpose of showing the stitches in the photo, a contrasting color is used.

Place the wire in the fold of the brim. Because the wire is already joined together on both ends, it must be pinned in place before sewing. It is very easy to pull the straw without realizing it while you are sewing, and pinning will help to keep it even.

Mark the center back where the joiner is located with a pin. Bump up your needle to the wire to ensure that the wire is tight inside the fold. Be sure that both straw layers stay together and that the wire stays in the fold as close to the edge as possible as it is being sewn in. Whipstitch around the wire. Do this two or three times to secure the first stitch. Move your needle ¹/₄" over and sew another whipstitch. Repeat this process all around.

Trim the excess straw as close as possible to the line you sewed without cutting into your stitches.

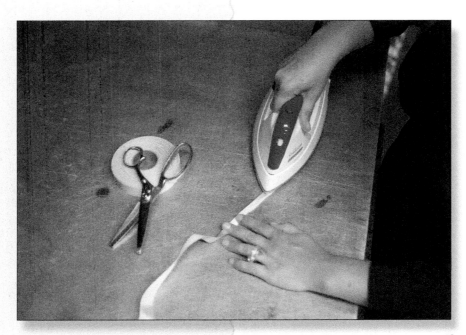

Ironing Petersham Trim in Half

Trim. Turn your iron on and set it to the cotton setting. We will be using Petersham for the trim. Measure the Petersham around the edge of the brim, adding 2" so it can be folded under at the end for a nice, finished look. Cut the Petersham with pinking shears to keep it from unraveling. Fold the Petersham in half lengthwise and iron in the crease. As you sew the trim on, you can bump up the fold to the edge of the brim, to ensure that the Petersham lies evenly on both sides of the brim edge.

Sew. Sew the ironed Petersham over the brim by hand. Using the sewing machine might cause the blocked hat to lose its shape. Start at the center back, and using a thread that matches the color of the Petersham, tack down both ends. Grab the edges of the Petersham on both sides by sewing through one side and coming out the other side. Use small stitches so they do not show.

When you get to about 2" before the end, fold the Petersham under, and overlap the starting point with it. Complete the sewing over the folded end.

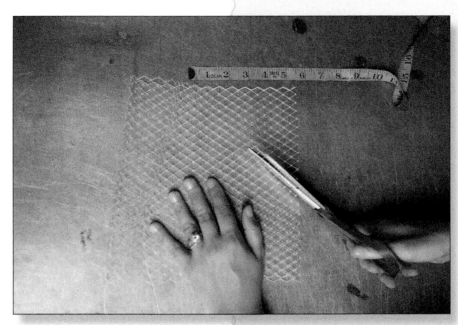

Cutting Corners of the Folded Veiling

PART 2—FEATHER FLOWER

See the "Making a Feather Flower" project on page 113 to learn how to make the feather flower for this hat. The sample uses the technique for the last three layers—the center only—of the sample.

Once the flower is made, set it aside. We will add this to the fascinator at the end.

PART 3—VEILING

Prepare. The veiling in the sample is 9" Russian veiling for a birdcage veil. A birdcage veil covers the wearer's eyes and ends at the sides of the face. For a veil that covers the face completely, an 18" veiling width should be used. Any type of veiling can be used in this project.

Measure the length of the veil you want. For a veil that ends around the sides of the face, cut a piece 20" in length.

Cut. Lay the veiling flat on the table and steam out any creases or folds. Fold the veiling in half widthwise. Starting from a top corner on the edge without the fold, measure 5" from the corner down and 5" from the corner across. Make a mark in both places. Use a ruler and tailor's chalk to ensure a straight line, or eyeball it and cut from one mark to the other. You are cutting a triangle shape out of the corner of the veiling. Unfold the veiling. There is now a triangle shape missing from both of the top corners of the veiling.

Sewing a Running Stitch Along Veiling Edge

Sew. Thread a needle with a double strand matching the color of the veiling. You are going to sew a running stitch from the bottom right corner all the way around the top edge to the bottom left corner. Do not sew along the bottom edge of the veiling. This is the part of the veil that will cover the face.

Make a knot in the thread to start so the thread stays put while you are sewing the running stitch. Russian veiling has dots on it that can be used to sew through. Use a running stitch every $1/2$". The veiling will begin to gather as you sew. When you reach the bottom left corner, gather the veiling until it measures about 3" across the top, keeping the sides even. Secure with a knot.

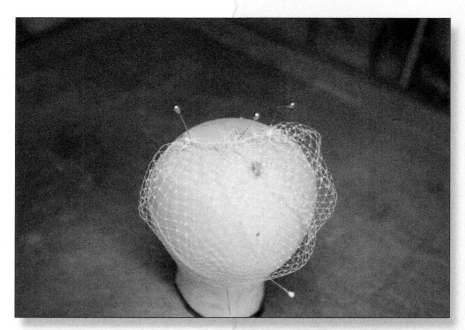

Gathered Veiling on Dummy Head

Placement. Pin the finished straw base to a dummy head to keep it secure while you place the veiling on it.

Hold the gathered veiling up to the base. Decide where you would like it placed; center front, or maybe more to one side? Do you want the veiling to go over one eye, or both? Pin the gathered top edge of the veiling to the base. Try it on in the mirror to be sure it is exactly as you want it, and adjust if needed. Tack the gathered veiling to the straw base, leaving the front of the veiling loose so it can be adjusted when worn.

Embellish. Place the hat with the veiling back on the dummy head. With the veiling tacked in place, position your completed feather flower on the fascinator over the veiling. The flower should cover the gather of the veiling at the top. When it is in position, pin the flower down using the felt tabs on the bottom and sew it by hand to the straw base.

Completed Elastic

Elastic. The elastic used for this project has metal ends for the purpose of adding it to a hat. The elastic sits behind the ears, across the back of the head under the hair. Hold the fascinator up to your head while looking into the mirror. When it is positioned where you want it, put your index finger behind one ear, and go straight up to the hat. Imagine the elastic going down from the base to directly behind that ear. Place a pin in the base to mark it. This is where the first end of the elastic is going to go. From the inside of the base, poke one of the metal ends through the straw, just above the Petersham trim. The metal end should be on the outside of the base. Following the Petersham trim, poke the metal back through to the inside of the base $1/2$" toward the back of the head. Keep close to the Petersham trim to hide the elastic.

Flip the hat upside down. Place a pin on the base directly opposite the first end. Starting from the inside of the base, poke through just above the Petersham trim. Following the Petersham trim, poke the metal back through to the inside of the base $1/2$" toward the back of the head. Try on the fascinator to be sure it is placed correctly.

Tack down the wire ends of the elastic on the inside of the base. Use a double strand of thread the same color as the straw, and whipstitch around the metal end to secure it to the straw base. If you do not do this, the metal ends can easily get caught in your hair.

You now have completed a beautiful bridal headpiece.

Fun Facts

Ancient Greeks and Romans thought the veil protected the bride from evil spirits. Brides have worn veils ever since.

Horsehair Fascinator

Horsehair is a fun, playful material that makes fascinating fascinators! These small headpieces are perfect when you want to add extra pizzazz to your outfit. Imagine wearing this fascinator to a holiday party or to the theater.

In this project, you will be working with horsehair, also called crinoline—one of my favorite materials. There are so many things you can sculpt with horsehair to create beautiful headpieces. Horsehair comes in many variations, and I encourage you to try different types. For the sample, a 6" plain horsehair was used.

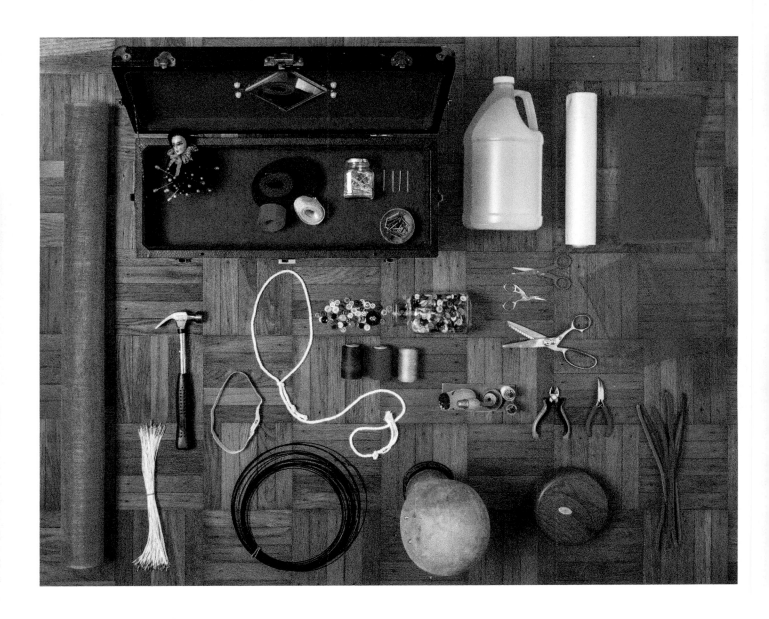

WHERE TO BUY:

Sinamay – Jolie Femmes

Horsehair – Judith M Millinery

Elastic – Judith M Millinery

Millinery wire and joiners –
   Judith M Millinery

Petersham – Jolie Femmes

Tools and Materials

Wooden kitchen bowl

Dummy head

Sinamay

1 yard of 6" horsehair in a solid
   color

Measuring tape

Pipe cleaners for beauty marks

Plastic wrap (Press'n Seal
   recommended)

Water bin

Hot water

Towel

Straw sizing

Squirt bottle for sizing

Steamer

Elastic for crown

Hammer

Nails or millinery tacks

Scissors

Thread

Needle

Pins

1 yard of $7/8$" Petersham

Iron

18–21 gauge millinery wire

Wire joiner

Pliers

Wire cutters

Superglue gel

Pinking sheers

Elastic for fascinator

Button

Soaking Sinamay

PART 1—BASE

Prepare. Cover the kitchen bowl with plastic wrap to protect it from dyes and water, keeping your block in good condition for years to come. This also prevents the straw from sticking to the block.

Measure out the amount of sinamay that you will be using on your block. Two layers of sinamay are used for this hat. This is the norm in the industry. Two layers are used to provide strength and durability to the hat. One layer would not be sturdy enough.

Lay your roll of sinamay over the block so that there are 3" of excess sinamay all around. Cut. Repeat for the second layer.

Soak. Fill the water bin with enough hot water to cover both layers of straw when submerged.

Soak both layers of straw in the hot water. Move the straw around in the water bin as it soaks to ensure all parts of the straw are saturated. Soak for 10 to 15 minutes.

Both Layers of Sinamay Lying Cross-Grained Over Block

Stretch. Turn your steamer on. Take one layer of straw out of the water and let it drip dry. Place it over the brim block and smooth it out with your hands. Then, take the second layer of straw out of the water, let it drip dry, and lay it cross-grained over the first layer. Smooth it out with your hands.

Place the elastic over the straw to hold it on the bowl. Then gently stretch the straw, starting with the bottom layer to get all of the pleats and bumps out of it. Do this all around the hat block. Repeat for the top layer. The straw can begin to dry as you work with it, so use the steamer to keep the fibers loose, allowing you to continue to stretch it.

Take your hand and slide it over the straw all around, if you feel a bump, that section needs adjusting. Look at the straw from all directions to be sure both straw layers are touching and there are no gaps. This can take a lot of practice. Straw will show every pleat and bump if not perfectly smoothed out.

Secure. Flip the block over. Since the block does not have a rope line, the straw is nailed or tacked to the bowl to secure it as it dries. It is important to nail in all four directions of the crown first, and then work in between. I refer to this as nailing at the north, south, east, and west points. Always nail in this manner because it is easy to pull the straw off center without realizing it.

Finally, the straw must be tightly secured during the drying process or it will shrink unevenly, creating waves in the fabric. It is very important to take your time with each step.

Sizing. When the straw is completely stretched and secure, spray the straw sizing over the blocked straw. Be sure to spray all areas including the edges where it is nailed in.

Let it dry overnight. It helps to put a fan on it and turn the block periodically.

Cut. Once the blocked straw is completely dry, it is ready to be trimmed before removing it from the block. First, remove the elastic and nails. Then, cut the excess straw all the way around approximately 1" from the brim edge. This does not need to be perfect because when the wire is sewn in, the excess straw will be cut away more precisely.

Carefully remove the blocked straw from the block. Slide your fingers under the straw and go around slowly, releasing it from the plastic and the block. Repeat this process until the straw can easily be removed without misshaping the blocked straw. Do not force it.

Wire. In order for the fascinator to stay stiff and keep the circular shape, we will be using 18–21 gauge millinery wire.

For this project, the wire is joined at both ends before it is sewn in, so the measurement must be exact. The wire is preset and pinned in place so that the fascinator maintains the upright, circular shape. When working with a small circular shape such as this one, it is best keep the natural curve of the wire from the coil.

Next, we are going to add a wire joiner to the end of the wire. Millinery wire is covered with two main threads, which can be easily removed by grabbing one of the threads and pulling it away from the wire. Remove the thread, exposing $1/2$" of the wire. Do the same with the second thread. Cut the loose thread off. Dab a very small amount of superglue gel onto the tip of the exposed wire. Then, place half of the wire joiner onto the wire and

Excess Straw Cut from Blocked Straw Base

Wire Joined at Both Ends with Joiner

use the pliers to clamp it closed. Repeat this process on the other end of the wire. When completed, your joined wire should fit perfectly in the folded edge of the straw.

Hand Sewing on Petersham Trim

Sew. It is difficult to machine sew the wire into a small base without deforming it. So for this project the wire will be sewn in by hand. Use a double strand of thread that is the same color as the straw.

Place the wire in the fold of the brim. Because the wire is already joined together on both ends, it must be pinned in place before sewing. It is very easy to pull the straw without realizing it while you are sewing, and pinning will help to keep it even.

Mark the center back where the joiner is located with a pin. Bump up your needle to the wire to ensure that the wire is tight inside the fold. Be sure that both straw layers stay together and that the wire stays in the fold as close to the edge as possible, as it is being sewn in. Whipstitch around the wire. Do this 2 or 3 times to secure the first stitch. Move your needle 1/4" over and sew another whipstitch. Repeat this process all around.

Trim the excess straw as close as possible to the line you sewed without cutting into your stitches.

Trim. Turn your iron on and set it to cotton. We will be using Petersham for the trim. Measure the Petersham around the edge of the brim, adding 2" so it can be folded under at the end for a nice, finished look. Cut the Petersham with pinking shears to keep it from unraveling. Fold the Petersham in half lengthwise and iron in the crease. As you sew the trim on, you can bump up the ironed edge to the edge of the brim, to ensure that the Petersham lies evenly on both sides of the brim edge.

90

Measuring Horsehair

Sew. Sew the ironed Petersham over the brim by hand. This is done for the same reason we put the wire in by hand. Using the machine might cause the blocked hat to lose its shape. Start at the center back, and using a thread that matches the color of the Petersham, tack down both ends. Grab the edges of the Petersham on both sides by sewing through one side and coming out the other side. Use small stitches so they do not show.

When you get to about 2" before the end, fold the Petersham under and overlap the starting point with it. Complete the sewing over the folded end.

PART 2—HORSEHAIR

Prepare. Use your dummy head as a base upon which to create your horsehair piece. You will be working with the horsehair in its original state, so there is no need to cover the dummy head. You will need pins to keep the horsehair in place while you work.

Cut. Cut off one yard of horsehair. Follow the next steps to make the form in the sample, or play and sculpt what your heart desires.

Horsehair Gathered and Tied Off

Finishing the Edges of the Horsehair

Gather. There is a thread that runs along one edge of the horsehair. When this thread is pulled from either end, the horsehair will gather. Pull CAREFULLY from each end, because if the thread breaks, then you will have to create your own thread by weaving it in and out of the horsehair.

Once you have pulled the horsehair thread from both ends, tie the thread together into a knot and cut off the excess thread.

Tie Off. Horsehair can be finished on the ends in a few different ways. You can leave it unfinished for a raw, frayed look. An even more frayed look can be achieved by rubbing your fingers back and forth on the ends to further separate the horsehair strands. For a clean, finished look, as in the sample, the ends are tied off.

Thread a needle with a double strand the same color as the horsehair. Fold one end of the horsehair in half; then fold it in half again. Take your needle and go through your double thread, so that you start off with the thread around the Horsehair. Start by wrapping the thread around the end of the horsehair several times, keeping at least 1" away from the edge so the thread doesn't slip off. You want to be as far from the edge as you can—at least 1", or the thread can slip off. Once you have wrapped the thread around the end, sew through the horsehair where it is wrapped, and tie it off. Repeat this on the other end. Cut off any excess horsehair $1/2$" from where it is tied off.

Sculpting Horsehair Atop Straw Base

Sculpt. Place your straw base on the dummy head. Pin one of the tied ends of the horsehair to the top of the base. Sculpt the horsehair by moving it back and forth, flipping it around, and twisting it.

For this hat design, I pinned down one of the tied ends, and twisted the other end into a circle. I then took the outside layer of the horsehair and flipped it inside out, creating a nice circular motion. Once you have achieved your desired look, tuck the other tied end under so that it is hidden, and pin it into the dummy head.

Sew. Thread a needle with a double strand. Now, with NEW pins, re-pin your shaped horsehair directly to the straw base, remov-

ing the old pins from the dummy head as you go. This will ensure that your creation does not shift.

Before taking the hat off the dummy head, be sure you have your needle threaded and ready to go. If you forget to do this, your creation can lose its form as you try to prepare the needle. Carefully take the hat off the dummy head, and tack the horsehair to the straw base, starting with the tied ends and making sure those are secure. Then, work around the horsehair and tack where you have pins.

Embellish. The sample is finished with a button at the center, but feel free to add whatever embellishment you choose.

Cutting Pipe Cleaners

The sample is further embellished with beauty marks made out of pipe cleaners With wire cutters, cut a pipe cleaner of your desired color into ³/₄" pieces.

Pin your hat back on the dummy head and decide where you want to place the beauty marks. As you add the beauty marks, take care not to snag the horsehair, as this will cause a run that cannot be repaired. Carefully push one end of a ³/₄" piece through the horsehair, push the other end through about ¹/₄" away. When both ends of the pipe cleaner are on the same side of the horsehair, fold them over each other against the horsehair.

Fun Facts

Another word for horsehair is crinoline. Crinoline has come very far since it first appeared in 1830. Crinoline was originally made with real horsehair that was woven with cotton or linen and used to create big hoop skirts for women. Today, horsehair is typically made with variations of nylon, cotton, and straw, and is often used in millinery.

Applying Pipe Cleaners to Horsehair

Elastic. The elastic used for this project has metal ends for the purpose of adding it to a hat. The elastic sits behind the ears, across the back of the head under the hair. Hold the fascinator up to your head while looking into the mirror. When it is positioned it where you want it, put your index finger behind one ear, and go straight up to the hat. Imagine the elastic going down from the base to directly behind that ear. Place a pin in the base to mark it. This is where the first end of the elastic is going to go. From the inside of the base, poke one of the metal ends through the straw, just above the Petersham trim. The metal end should be on the outside of the base. Following the Petersham trim, poke the metal back through to the inside of the base $1/2$" toward the back of the head. Keep close to the Petersham trim to hide the elastic.

Flip the hat upside down. Place a pin on the base directly opposite the first end. Starting from the inside of the base, poke through just above the Petersham trim and come out the other side. Following the Petersham trim, poke the metal back through to the inside of the base $1/2$" toward the back of the head. Try on the fascinator to be sure the elastic is placed correctly.

Tack down the wire ends of the elastic on the inside of the base. Use a double strand of thread the same color as the straw, and whipstitch around the metal end to secure it to the straw base. If you do not do this, the metal ends can easily get caught in your hair.

Your horsehair fascinator is completed! Imagine the possibilities you can create with horsehair!

Jinsin Fascinator

If you enjoy making sculptural headpieces, you will enjoy working with jinsin. It can be used to create large or small hats or to add wonderful embellishments to a current piece.

Jinsin is a beautiful, versatile material that can form wonderful loops, bows, and circular shapes. Let your mind and hands do the creating. Follow the steps to make the sample project, or add your own jinsin creation to the base.

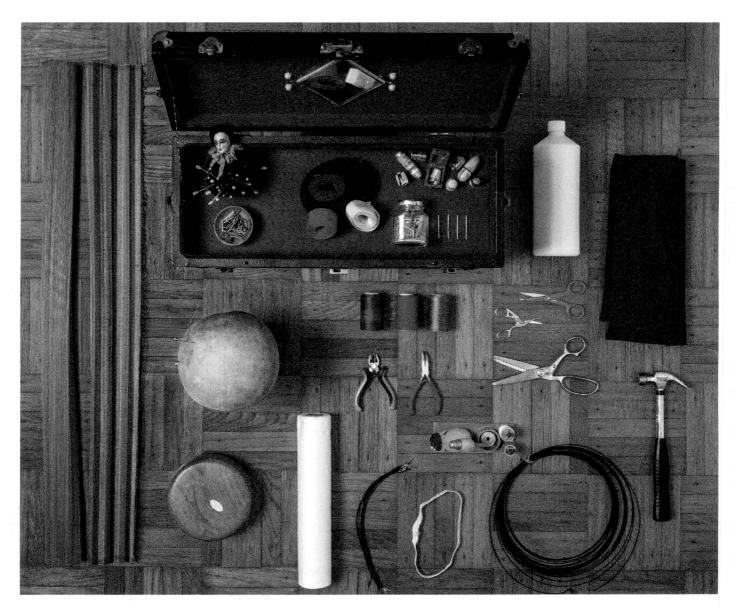

WHERE TO BUY:

Jinsin – Torb & Reiner

Flat felt wool –
  Judith M Millinery

Elastic – Judith M Millinery

Millinery wire and joiners –
  Judith M Millinery

Petersham – Jolie Femmes

Wooden kitchen bowl block	Iron
Dummy head	Thimble
$1/2$ yard each of solid and striped jinsin	Towel
$1/2$ yard of flat felt wool	Steamer
Hot water	Scissors
Water bin	Pins
Plastic wrap (Press'n Seal recommended)	Thread
Squirt bottle for sizing	Needle
Wool sizing	18–21 gauge millinery wire – 21 gauge recommended
Hammer	Superglue gel
Nails or millinery tacks	Wire joiner
Elastic for wool	Wire cutters
1 yard of $7/8$" Petersham	Pliers
Pinking shears	Sewing machine
	Elastic for fascinator

PART 1—BASE

Prepare. Cover the bowl with plastic wrap to protect it from any dyes in the material and to keep the wool from sticking to the block.

Get your steamer ready to go, and have elastic, nails/tacks, hammer, and wool sizing in your squirt bottle at hand.

Measure out the amount of flat felt wool that you will be using. Only one layer of wool is used. Lay the wool over the hat block, keeping in mind that you want to cover the sides of the bowl, too. Make sure you have about 3" of excess wool all the way around. It is better to have too much wool than not enough.

Soak. Fill the water bin with enough hot water to cover the material when submerged. Soak the wool in the hot water. Move the material around in the water bin as it soaks to ensure all parts of the wool are saturated. The wool should begin to feel softer and looser. Let it soak for approximately fifteen minutes.

Soaking causes the wool fibers to relax and open up. As the wool dries over the block, the fibers close to maintain the shape in which it has been formed.

Sizing. Turn on the steamer. Remove the wool from the bin and gently squeeze out the excess water. Do not wring out the water. Gently squeeze the wool.

If there is a right side and wrong side of the wool, spray it on the wrong side, reaching the center and all edges. Rub the wool back and forth in your hands to massage the sizing into the wool. Once that is completed, lay the wool over the hat block.

Soaking Wool

Spraying Sizing on Wool

Stretch. Place the elastic over the wool. Stretch the wool over the hat block in all directions. This is where your steamer comes in handy. As you work with the wool, use the steamer to keep the fibers loose, allowing you to continue to stretch it. Your goal is to get all of the pleats, wrinkles, bumps, and bubbles out so the wool is completely smooth.

Excess Wool Cut from Blocked Wool

Secure. Flip the block over. Since the block does not have a rope line, the wool is nailed or tacked to the bowl to secure it as it dries. It is important to nail in all four directions of the block first, and then work in between. I refer to this as nailing at the north, south, east, and west points. Always nail in this manner because it is easy to pull the wool off center without realizing it.

Once secured, allow to dry overnight.

Cut. Once the blocked wool is completely dry, it is ready to be trimmed before it is removed from the block. First, remove the elastic and nails. Then, cut the excess wool all the way around, approximately 1" from the edge. This does not need to be perfect because when the wire is sewn in, the excess wool will be cut away more precisely.

Carefully remove the blocked wool from the kitchen block. Slide your fingers under the wool and go around slowly, releasing it from the plastic and the block. Repeat this process until the wool can easily be removed without misshaping it. Do not force it.

Wire. In order for the fascinator to stay stiff and keep the circular shape, we will be using 18–21 gauge millinery wire.

Hand Sewing Wire into Wool Edge

For this project, the wire is joined at both ends before it is sewn in, so the measurement must be exact. The wire is preset and pinned in place so that the fascinator maintains the upright, circular shape. When working with a small circular shape such as this one, it is best to keep the natural curve of the wire from the coil.

Next, we are going to add the wire joiner to ends of the wire. Millinery wire is covered with two main threads that can be easily removed by grabbing one of the threads and pulling it away from the wire. Remove the thread, exposing ¹/₂" of the wire. Do the same with the second thread. Cut the loose thread off. Dab a very small amount of superglue gel onto the tip of the exposed wire. Then, place half of the wire joiner onto the wire and use the pliers to clamp it closed. Repeat this process on the other end of the wire. When complete, your joined wire should fit perfectly in the folded edge of the wool.

Sew. It is difficult to machine sew wire into a small base without deforming it. So for this project the wire will be sewn in by hand. Use a double strand of thread that is the same color as the wool. For the purpose of showing the stitches in the photo, a contrasting color was used.

Place the wire in the fold of the brim. Because the wire is already joined together on both ends, it must be pinned in place before sewing. It is very easy to pull the wool without realizing it while you are sewing and pinning will help to keep it even.

Mark the center back where the joiner is located with a pin. Bump up your needle to the wire to ensure that the wire is tight inside the fold. Be sure that the wire stays in the fold as close to the edge as possible as it is being sewn in. Whipstitch around the wire two or three times to secure the first stitch. Move your needle ¹/₄" over and sew another whipstitch. Repeat this process all around.

Trim the excess wool as close as possible to the line you sewed without cutting into your stitches.

Completed Petersham Trim Along the Wool Edge

Trim. Turn your iron on and set it to cotton. We will be using Petersham as the trim. Measure the Petersham around the edge of the brim, adding 2" so it can be folded under at the end for a nice, finished look. Cut the Petersham with pinking shears to keep it from unraveling. Fold the Petersham in half lengthwise and iron in the crease. As you sew the trim on, you can bump up the ironed edge to the edge of the brim, to ensure that the Petersham lies evenly on both sides of the brim edge.

Sew. Sew the ironed Petersham over the brim by hand. Using the sewing machine might cause the blocked hat to lose its shape. Start at center back, and using a thread that matches the color of the Petersham, tack down both ends. Grab the edges of the Petersham on both sides by sewing through one side and coming out the other side. Use small stitches so they do not show.

When you get to about 2" before the end, fold the Petersham under and overlap the starting point with it. Complete sewing over the folded end.

The Jinsin Pieces Cut to 7" Long

PART 2—JINSIN

Prepare. Cover the dummy head with plastic wrap. The sample uses 2 colors of jinsin—one solid color, and one striped. As you work with jinsin, strands of the bamboo will unravel from the cotton threads. This is normal. You can either discard these pieces, or keep them for later and use them as part of your embellishment. Removing many of these loose strands creates a wonderful frayed look. In order to keep the pieces from continuing to unravel, fold over the edge and sew it down. For a finished edge, this needs to be done before the sculpting process begins.

Sculpt the jinsin, on the dummy head and not on the wool base that you just created. The jinsin has to be saturated the whole time it is sculpted to keep the fibers from breaking and this would ruin the wool base. So the jinsin is sewn to the base once it has dried completely.

Cut. Cut two pieces of jinsin each 7" long. When cutting the jinsin, follow the grain of the bamboo. Your scissors will slide easily between the fibers. Cutting across the fibers will make a jagged edge and it will be difficult to achieve the effect you want. If you do create a jagged edge, start over and cut along the grain.

Frayed Edge on Jinsin

Fray. Fray one of the 7" jinsin pieces. The pieces of the bamboo are already trying to separate. Continue the process by removing bamboo strands from both sides. Alternate sides to be sure the fraying is even on both ends. Remove strands until there is a 3"–4" band of solid bamboo in the center, or the length desired.

Soak. Prepare your steamer and hot water bin. Soak the frayed layer of jinsin in the hot water for 15–20 minutes. This will saturate the fibers so they don't break as they are manipulated.

Fun Facts

Waltraud Reiner, owner of Torb and Reiner in Melbourne, Australia, is the brilliant milliner who introduced jinsin to the millinery world in 2005. Torb and Reiner, one of the leaders in the millinery market, works with the manufacturer to create exclusive, custom jinsin colors. Their staff has over a hundred years of combined millinery experience.

Sculpted Frayed Jinsin Piece on Dummy Head

Sculpt. Follow the steps, or create your own look.

Measure the circumference of your finished wool base. Using the frayed jinsin layer, you will be creating a circle that is 2" smaller than the wool base so it can sit atop of the wool base at a slant.

Place your covered dummy head in front of you. You will also need your pins to help hold the jinsin on the dummy head.

Let the jinsin drip dry.

Fold the frayed jinsin in half so both frayed ends are facing down. If it is too long, then cut off one end so it is 2" shorter in circum- ference than your base. Create a circle with the jinsin, tuck the raw ends underneath the circle, and pin.

Use your steamer to prevent the jinsin from drying out. This will be evident if, when you are working with it, the fibers create more of a bend than a curve. Once the fibers are broken, they cannot go back to their original state. So, take care that the jinsin is constantly saturated and is easy to sculpt in a circle without creasing it.

Once it is sculpted into a circle, set it aside.

Prepare. Create a finished end in both sides of the second piece of jinsin. Fold one edge over $1/2$" and then $1/2$" again so the raw edge is completely hidden. Use your sewing machine to sew a straight stitch along the edge. Do the same on the other side of the raw edge of the jinsin. You now have the 7" jinsin with a clean, finished edge on each side.

Soak. Soak the piece in a hot water bin for 15–20 minutes. Then let it drip dry when you remove it from the bin.

Sculpting the Second Jinsin Piece Inside the Frayed Jinsin Circle

Sculpt. You will be sculpting directly over the circle of the first jinsin piece. Start in the center of the frayed circle, and pin one end of the second piece to the dummy head. Then, form a circle along the inside of the frayed circle. Spiral up a bit to make a second circle. Tuck under the other loose end and pin. When making shapes with the jinsin, pin as you go to maintain the shape. Once the jinsin is pinned down, you can play with it by pulling each edge apart to expand and flare it. You can also push the edges together in places to vary the effect.

When you have the look you want, let the pieces dry for a couple of hours. It helps to put on a fan.

Secure. Once the pieces are dry, reposition the pins so that they hold the shape without going into the dummy head, removing each one from the head without shifting what you created. Then, place the wool base back on the dummy head and pin down.

Sew the ends of the frayed circle together by hand. Use a double strand of thread to match the jinsin and sew along the grain of the jinsin. The thread will fall between the jinsin strands and be hidden. Jinsin can be a tough material to sew through, so you may need to use a thimble, especially when going through multiple layers. Once secured, place the piece on the wool base and position it to sit at an angle. You may also want to take both pieces to a mirror to play with the positioning. Sew the frayed jinsin to the wool base.

Position the second layer of jinsin inside the frayed circle and tack it down, starting with the ends and tacking where needed.

Jinsin doesn't need a lot of embellishment, but if you would like to add the strands of Jinsin that you removed earlier, or any other embellishment, now would be the time.

Completed Elastic

Elastic. The elastic used for this project has metal ends for the purpose of adding it to a hat. The elastic sits behind the ears, across the back of the head under the hair. Hold the fascinator up to your head while looking into the mirror. When it is positioned where you want it, put your index finger behind one ear, and go straight up to the hat. Imagine the elastic going down from the base to directly behind that ear. Place a pin in the base to mark it. This is where the first end of the elastic is going to go. From the inside of the base, poke one of the metal ends through the jinsin, just above the Petersham trim. The metal end should be on the outside of the base. Following the Petersham trim, poke the metal back through to the inside of the base $1/2$" toward the back of the head. Keep close to the Petersham trim to hide the elastic. Flip the hat upside down. Place a pin on the base directly opposite the first end. Starting from the inside of the base, poke through just above the Petersham trim and come out the other side. Following the Petersham trim, poke the metal back through to the inside of the base $1/2$" toward the back of the head. Try on the fascinator to be sure the elastic is placed correctly.

Tack down the wire ends of the elastic on the inside of the base. Use a double strand of thread the same color as the straw, and whipstitch around the metal end to secure it to the straw base. If you do not do this, the metal ends can easily get caught in your hair.

You have just completed your jinsin creation. With jinsin, there are so many possibilities, and I hope you will experiment to see what more it can do.

Embellishments

Embellishment
(em-bel-ish-muhnt) n.
A decoration
or adornment
applied to a hat.

Embellishments can be made from all types of materials. The next two projects, making a feather flower and hatpins, will help take your creativity to the next level. Once you know how to make feather flowers, you may never buy another one again. Do you have an old brooch or earring of your mother's? You can turn beautiful old treasures into a functional hatpin to be worn on a hat, purse, or lapel.

Vintage flowers also make great embellishments. If you have some stored away or find some in your favorite thrift store, you can use them to embellish a hat. Don't pass them up if they are a bit wrinkled, as they can easily be fixed with a little steam. Steam each flower individually, petal by petal. You will be surprised by the life that you can bring back to an old flower with a little steam.

Working with Feathers

Working with feathers can be a lot of fun. Following the easy steps on pages 114–121, you will learn how to prepare feathers to create beautiful feather flower combinations. Once you complete this project, you'll want to experiment with different ways to create your own feather patterns.

The Feather Body. The bottom of the feather is the quill. If you follow the quill upwards into the feather, it becomes the shaft. The top of the feather is the feather tip. The little individual feathers that create the whole feather are called barbs.

A feather has a front and back. The front of the feather is smooth, and the shaft is smooth and nicely curved. If you flip the feather over, you will notice that the shaft has a tiny line or split from the quill to the feather tip. It is important to be aware of the front and back when cutting and curling the feathers.

Cutting a Feather. Use a sharp pair of small scissors. The smaller the point at the end of the scissors, the better because you want to be able to get as close to the shaft as possible when cutting. Scissors with thicker points at the end make it more challenging. Cut a

feather upside down, or with the quill facing upwards. This way you are going against the flow of the feathers, so it is easier to cut into them without the feathers pushing against the scissors and interfering. Try cutting a section of feathers with the feather right side up and upside down to see the difference.

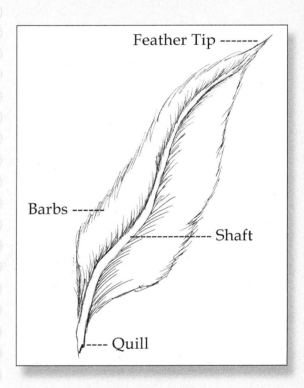

Feather created by Illustrator: David Green, aka Starvin-Artist

Removing Feathers by Hand. When removing feathers by hand, hold the feather right side up with the feather tip facing up. When you pull the barbs off, you pull them downward towards the quill, going against the natural flow of the feathers. This will remove the barbs from the shaft completely.

Curling Feathers. What is fascinating about feathers is that anything you can do with your hair, you can pretty much do with a feather. You can curl it with a curling iron or a flat iron, spray it, wet it, and dye it. Always curl the feather going towards the back, following the natural bend of the feather. Never force the feather to bend in a different direction because you might break it.

A curling iron will give the feather nice curlicues. Just like hair, the tighter and closer you curl the feather on the curling iron, the tighter the curl will appear in the feather. The more you spread the feather out around the curling iron, the looser the curl. Different size curling irons will also create different effects.

The flat iron is a tool gives you a lot of control over the amount of curl you put into the feather. Starting to curl the feather from the quill results in tight curls, starting from the feather tip or the middle of the feather results in more gradual curls. Practice in order to learn how to create the exact curls you want.

Buying Feathers. Feathers are sold in a couple of different ways. They can be found sewn on a strand, which is typically available in 3" increments. They can also be purchased loose by the pound or ounce, as are the feathers used in the sample. Buying the feathers in bulk gets you the greatest quantity of feathers for your money.

Organizing the Feathers. When you get your pack of feathers, you will notice that all of the feathers do not look the same. You will find that there are about three distinct lengths among the feathers. Some of the feathers are nice and full, while others look somewhat chewed up with barbs missing or distorted. This is normal. When making the feather flowers, you will want to choose the best feathers you have. You can throw the others away or keep them for a different project. The feather shafts may also be different strengths. As you are working with feathers, they may break. This, too, is normal. Just throw that feather away and get a new one.

Making a Feather Flower "Crazy Legs"

For this project you want a quarter pound bag—approximately fifty feathers—of goose satinettes or goose nagoire. The size of your flower project will determine the number of feathers that you will use. Two different colors are used in the sample. You can also make it with only one color.

Goose feathers are wide and full of life, and I prefer them for flowers. You can cut into them and strip away feathers to really show off your design. You can use the techniques in this book with other types of feathers, but if the barbs are narrower, you will have a different end result. Again, once you learn these techniques, try them on different feathers to reach your own conclusion about what works best for you.

This is a two-part feather flower. The first three layers, the outside of the flower, uses one manipulating technique. A second technique is used for the final 3 layers to finish the flower. The flower for the Bridal Fascinator on page 73 is made using the second technique.

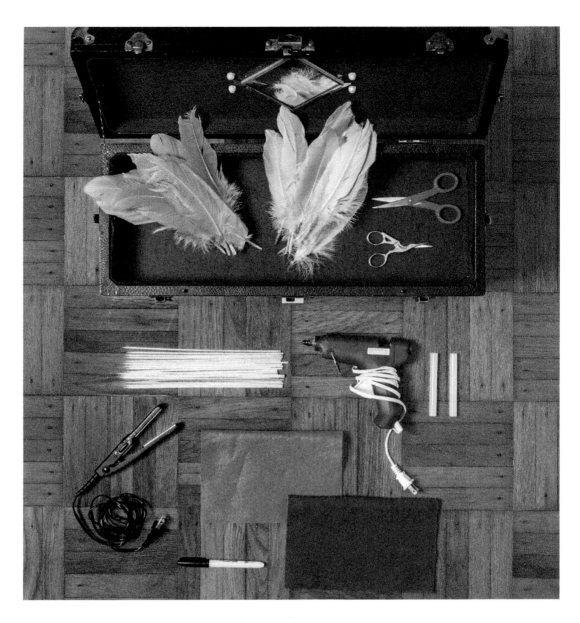

WHERE TO BUY:

Feathers –
   Moonlight Feathers

Tools and Materials

Feather Flowers: ¼ lb. bag of goose satinettes or goose nagoire. (24 feathers in each color are needed for this project)

Travel size flat iron

Small piece of flat felt wool

Wooden poker (pointed stick for applying the feather)

Black marker for polka dots

Scrap paper

Hot glue sticks

Hot glue gun

Scissors

114

Felt Pad with Tab and Organized Feathers

PART 1—OUTER FLOWER

Prepare. Heat up the glue gun and flat iron and set them aside.

Determine how big you want your flower to be, to determine how big the wool circle base should be. The bigger the wool circle you make, the bigger the flower. For the sample project, which is a 7"–8" flower, cut a 2" circle out of flat felt wool. Then cut a wool tab 2" long by ¹/₂" wide.

Cut two ¹/₂" slits in the center of the circle, ¹/₂" apart. Slide the tab through the slits so both ends stick out on one side, and glue the center of the tab to the wool circle. The tabs will be sewn to the hat to fasten the flower on. Once the tab is glued, place the circle in front of you with the tab facing down.

The flower is made with six layers of feathers. You will make one layer at a time from start to finish, starting with the outside of the flower and working toward the center. Each layer consists of eight feathers.

Begin by organizing the feathers by width. The widest feathers will be used in the first layer with the feathers getting narrower as we work toward the center.

Determine the length of feather that you want to use. If you want a large feather flower upon completion, then you want to start with long feathers and gradually get shorter. The first layer in the sample flower uses feathers 4¹/₂" long.

Cut. Cut eight of the widest feathers 4¹/₂" inches long. Because this is the outside of the feather flower, these will be the longest feathers used. The feathers will be cut ¹/₂" shorter for each successive layer.

Cut the feathers by placing your scissors as close as you can to the shaft, and snip off the rest of the feather. Lay the remaining feathers face up with the slit in the shaft on the table ready for use.

Curl. Hold the quill of one feather between your thumb and index finger, with the back of the feather facing you. With the flat iron in your other hand, start from the quill and slide the flat iron up the shaft, to the feather tip. As you do this, curl the feather inward towards you to give it a slight curve. Repeat for the remaining seven feathers in this layer.

Curling Feathers with Flat Iron

Manipulate. When the 8 feathers are curled, hold the feather tip of one feather with your thumb and forefinger. Starting from the top, slide the thumb and forefinger of your other hand down the shaft all the way to the quill. This will scramble the barbs into what I call crazy legs. Repeat with the remaining seven feathers in this layer.

Sliding Fingers Down Feather to Scramble the Barbs

Remove. We will now remove parts of the feather by stripping them away by hand. You want to strip away the same amount of feathers on both sides so that they match.

Start about 1" from the feather tip, and work on one side of the shaft. Separate the barbs, grab the feathers and pull down removing $1/2$"-1" of feathers, pulling them off the shaft. This leaves a gap along the shaft with no barbs. Repeat on the opposite side.

Leaving about 1" of barbs intact, move down the shaft and strip away another $1/2$"–1" segment of barbs. Repeat on the opposite side. Be sure to leave barbs intact at the bottom of the feather. You now have a feather with barbs at the top, then a gap where barbs were stripped, another section of intact barbs at the middle, a second gap, and then a section of intact barbs at the bottom.

You will now have a feather that is slightly curled, with crazy legs, and two gaps on each side of the shaft. Repeat with the remaining seven feathers in this layer.

Glue. Get your wool circle, glue gun, and wooden poker ready. Make sure the tab on the wool circle is facing down towards the table.

Removing Feathers by Hand on Each Side

Gluing Feather Onto Wool Pad with Wooden Poker

117

Three Layers of Completed Feathers

We will be gluing the feathers to the wool circle at the north, south, east, and west points. Start in these four corners and glue the other feathers between them.

Put a small dab of hot glue on the end of one feather. Place the feather on the edge of the wool circle, and use the wooden poker to hold down the end of the feather until it is secure. Do not use your finger. The glue will burn you, and it will hurt! Repeat this process at the remaining compass points. Glue the remaining four feathers between the first four, staying on the edge of the wool.

Repeat. Working one layer at a time, prepare two more groups of eight feathers for each layer. Cut each group of eight feathers ½" shorter than the previous layer. Curl each layer so that it curls further inward than the previous layer. When removing the barbs, the stripped and intact sections will be slightly smaller than the previous layer. The goal is to keep feathers intact on the top, middle, and bottom of the feather, so you may only remove ½" of barbs in the section. We are using the same feather technique with each layer, use your judgment to adjust for the shorter lengths.

There will be room in the center of the wool circle for the remaining layers, which use a different feather technique.

Removing One Side of the Feathers by Hand

PART 2—INNER FLOWER

Prepare. If you are making a two-color flower, use the second color for the remaining layers. The hot glue, flat iron, wooden poker, and a black marker are needed for this next phase.

Organize the feathers by length. You will be using the shorter length for the remaining layers. You will need three sets of eight feathers.

Cut. Cut the first eight feathers for the fourth layer ¹/₄″ shorter than the feathers in the previous layer, using the same method as for the first three layers. Lay the remaining feathers face up with the slit in the shaft on the table ready for use

Fun Facts

Birds are the only creatures that have feathers.

The average bird has between fifteen hundred and three thousand feathers.

So many birds were hunted and killed to provide feathers for ladies' hats in the early twentieth century that laws were enacted for the legal protection of birds in the UK and the U.S.

Creating Polka Dots on Feathers with a Marker

Remove. Remove the feathers first before curling them with the straight iron. Each feather will have one whole side stripped of feathers.

Hold the top of one feather with your thumb and forefinger and with your other hand, starting about $1/4$ of the way from the feather tip, grab the barbs on one side of the shaft, and pull down towards the quill, removing all the barbs along one side of the shaft. Discard what you remove. Now remove the feathers at the very top on the same side. Carefully using the same technique, pull the feathers downward to remove them. This is a little more challenging, so go slowly and eventually you will get it.

One entire side of the feather should be bare.

Repeat for the remaining seven feathers in this layer.

Curl. Curl each of the eight feathers with the flat iron. Continue to curl each layer further inward than the previous layer. The center feathers are curled completely to resemble a closed flower.

With the back of the feather facing you and your flat iron, start at the quill, and with a swooping motion, curl the feather towards the inside, all the way up to the feather tip. Repeat with the remaining seven feathers.

Manipulate. After you have curled all eight feathers, grab a piece of scrap paper and your black marker. Place the feathers on the scrap paper with the fronts facing you and make random black dots on each feather. This will make a fun, polka dot pattern.

Glueing Down the Fourth Layer of Feathers

Glue. Glue this layer to the wool pad in the same way as the previous layers, continuing to work towards the center.

This layer is almost in the center of the wool circle, so you will have room for one or two more layers.

Repeat. Repeat the process above, for the remaining layers, being sure to curl the last layer as tightly as possible so that it resembles a closed or slightly opening flower. To make a really tight curve, start very close to the base of the feather near the quill and curve inward with your iron.

Fill. Once the last layer is glued in, set your flower in front of you and slowly turn it in a circle. You will see areas that need additional feathers. Be sure to look at the flower from the top to the bottom and fill in any gaps you find.

When adding feathers, be sure to match the length, technique, and amount of curl to the other feathers in the layer.

Be very careful not to accidentally touch the surrounding feathers with the glue. It may be helpful for you to use one hand to spread the feathers so that you can glue easily in between them.

Once you have a beautiful, full feathered flower, it is ready to be sewn to the hat by the wool tabs.

Now you know how to create beautiful feather flowers. Practice these techniques, and come up with your own creations. The possibilities are endless! Imagine all of the different looking feather flowers you can make.

Hatpins

Hatpins are easy to make using lovely things that you have hidden away in your jewelry box—your mother's earring or an old brooch you never wear. A hatpin can be a great gift, especially if you incorporate something with sentimental value.

On one end of the hatpin is a pinhead, a flat piece of metal to keep any beads or other embellishments from slipping off. This is the tip of the hatpin to which embellishments are glued.

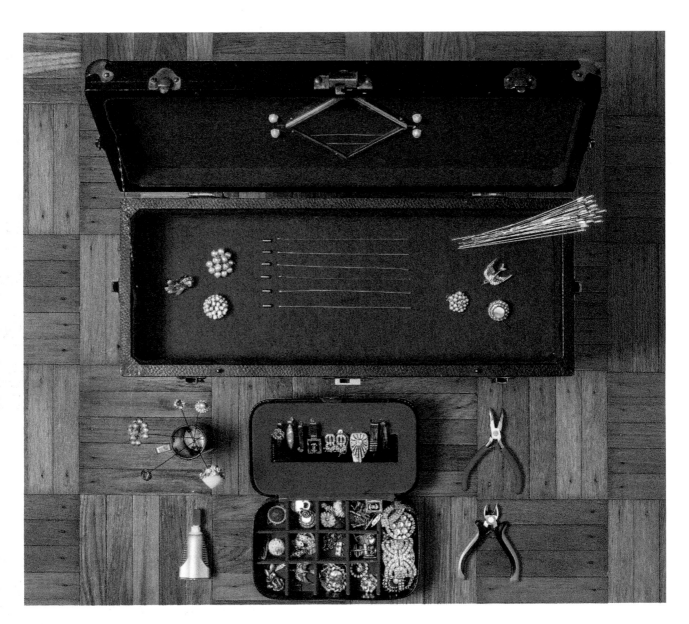

Tools and Materials

Hatpin stems
Superglue gel
Wire cutters

Pliers
Adornment

Fun Facts

According to the American Hatpin Society, hatpins have been used since the fifteenth
century. In the 1600s, Gloucestershire, a hatpin manufacturer, employed fifteen
hundred hatpin makers. Handmade hatpins were expensive, so only the wealthy could
afford them to hold their veils, wimples, and other headgear in place when the wind
blew. In 1832, a machine was invented in America, which could mass-produce hatpins,
making them more affordable. In 1908, laws were passed in America that limited the
length of hatpins, as there was a concern that suffragettes might use them as weapons.

Prepare. Look for an adornment with a flat surface or a small hole in the back where you can attach the pin-head. The hole or flat surface doesn't necessarily need to be in the center of the adornment as long as there is somewhere to easily attach the hatpin.

Many clip-on earrings have small holes on the back of them. I often look for a pair, or even a single earring, to use for this project.

Removing Earring Backing with Pliers

Remove. Choose the adornment that you are going to use. Look at the backing and decide if you will need to cut it off with a wire cutter. You can also take a pair of pliers, grab the backing on both sides and move it back and forth until it breaks off. Use the wire cutters to remove any small metal pieces that are left behind. Discard the backing.

BackingsRemoved from Earringa and Brooches

Placing Glue on Pinhead

Secure. Place the adornment upside down to expose the hole or flat surface. Put a dab of superglue gel at the end of the pinhead and stick it into the hole or flat surface.

Placing Pinhead on Brooch

Hold the hatpin straight up to dry. Stand up and look at it from above to be sure that the hatpin is straight up and down. Softly blow on the glue to help it dry. Let it dry undisturbed for about one to two hours before applying it to a hat. So, find a place to set it down.

Once it is completely dry, you have a beautiful, functional hatpin.

How to Care for Your Hat

It is important to take proper care of your hats. By following these simple tips, you will have fresh and vibrant hats for many years to come. Always keep the hat in a hatbox with acid-free tissue paper. Be sure that you use acid-free tissue as the acids in common tissue can turn yellow and eventually stain your hat.

If your brim flips down and you do not have a lot of embellishments on the hat, it is best to store the hat upside down to keep from crushing the brim.

If your brim flips up or you have a lot of embellishments such as feathers or flowers, then you will need to store your hat right side up.

Regardless of which direction your hat sits inside the box, fill the crown with tissue or a towel to keep it nice and round. Make sure the crown is not pushed in and there are

no dents or dimples. Over time, dimples can create a permanent mark on the crown or cause the hat to change shape. If there are embellishments on the hat, be sure not to bend them with the lid of the box. You can place tissue around embellishments, like flowers, to keep them from drooping. Do not put more than one hat in a hatbox. Over time, they will crush each other. If a hat becomes misshapen, it can sometimes be re-blocked by a milliner—but only if the straw or wool has not been torn or become brittle.

If your hat gets dust on it, or it becomes slightly dirty, gently go over it with a soft bristle brush to remove any dirt particles. If there is a slight stain, you can try a little water or steam and gently dab at it to remove any residue. If you have a bad stain on your hat, your local dry cleaner may be able to assist you.

Setting Up Your Hat Studio Workspace

Formé Millinery Hat Shop Windows

Whether you are setting up a workspace in your home, an outside studio, or storefront, there are some key factors to keep in mind as you plan.

Space. Though you may start out small with few tools and supplies, you will soon accumulate more, which will overtake your current space. So, eventually, you will want plenty of space. It is never fun when your finished product and materials start to take over, and you have no room to actually practice your craft. When I began hat making, I started in my home, and it soon took over the whole house. Needless to say, if you have other people living with you, they may not appreciate this. I soon moved into a much-needed storefront, with plenty of space to work and showcase my hats, and even some room to grow if needed. I am much happier, and so are my husband and my cats!

Lighting. The appropriate lighting is crucial, especially for sewing. Plan to have plenty of overhead lighting, as well as task lamps for close work. Different types of lighting like florescent lights or full-spectrum light can affect the way you see shades of color, so try to find the most natural light possible.

Comfortable Table and Chairs. You may be sitting as you work for many hours at a time, so it is very important to be able to relax and sit comfortably without straining your back or neck. Consider the height of the desk; can you easily sew at it? I prefer a chair with a back, as opposed to a stool. When I sit in a stool, I tend to slouch, which can cause discomfort to my back. I felt it was important to have a specific place to make my hats that was not my sewing desk. Because I was working with water and steam, I looked for a table that would not get easily ruined by these elements. I found a vintage table with a steel top and a drawer in which I could keep all my nails, pins, my hammer, and sizing close by for easy access.

Formé Millinery Sewing Station

Formé Millinery Organized Supplies

Formé Millinery Organized Hat Blocks

Formé Millinery Hat Shop—View from Work Station

Another key consideration is where to put all of your materials. I like organization, and I have all of my materials sorted by content. When I was in a smaller space, it was difficult to do this, and often I would come across a material that I didn't even realize I had. Being organized can save you money as well as time. If you have all the same content in one place, then you know exactly what you have, and you don't need to ask yourself, "Do I have that straw in black?" I separate and organize all of my straw, sinamay, parasisal, vintage straw, wools, jinsin, and horsehair. I have a section for my veiling and flowers. Even my beading is organized. If you do this right from the start, you will be happy later. It is just easier to function.

When I was looking for a retail hat shop, my first priority was to have plenty of room to display all of my hat collections. I wanted to have my workspace in the same location, so I set that up in the back of the store. If you are planning on having customers come to your workspace or store, you want to keep in mind how it will appear to your customers. First impressions are huge for people coming into your space for the first time. As a business owner, I want to portray professionalism at all times, so I keep my retail space and workspace tidy. When meeting a client for a custom hat, I will bring him or her into my work area so we can look over different types of materials and embellishments. Because I am organized, I can quickly grab colors of a certain type of material without wasting my customer's time trying to find things.

It is an incredible experience working one-on-one with clients, measuring their heads, picking out materials and embellishments, and creating hats specifically made just for them. It is also special for the client to see how the hats are made. They will often look through my hat blocks and my old trunk of trims. I provide a high level of service, and enjoy creating an experience for my clients by involving them in the hat-making process as much as they want. Some like coming back multiple times to watch the hat being made and transformed in front of their eyes!

My hat shop and workspace are filled with things that inspire me, such as pictures of old hats, vintage trims, inspirational sayings, vintage displays, and articles that I have been featured in. Make it your space to create and learn. I have included some pictures to show you how I have set up my space. I hope this too, inspires you to get creative and put together that special place for you to make hats.

Formé Millinery Hat Shop

Formé Millinery Hat Shop

Supplies

MILLINERY SUPPLY HOUSES
United States

Judith M Millinery *
www.judithm.com

Jolie Femmes *
www.joliefemmessupplies.com

Moonlight Feathers *
www.moonlightfeather.com

Manhatco
www.manhatco.com

Hat Supply
www.hatsupply.com

Australia

Torb & Reiner *
www.torbandreiner.com

United Kingdom

Parkin
www.parkinfabrics.co.uk

HAT BLOCK MAKERS
United Kingdom

Guy Morse-Brown*
www.hatblocks.co.uk

Hat Blocks Direct
www.hatblocksdirect.co.uk

Australia

Hat Blocks Australia
www.hatblocksbydesign.com.au

(*) Used in the hat projects throughout this book

Acknowledgements

I would like to thank all of the people involved in the making of this book: Natalie Warady, for writing the Foreword for this book, and who I met in the beginning of my career, during which she provided me with many words of encouragement; Steve Squall who is a genius when it comes to photography and shot ALL of the lovely photos throughout this book; Cassandra Mastropaolo, who was the perfect model that made my hats glow; Isidro Valencia, who is a brilliant makeup artist and hair stylist; Megan Wilde, the still life stylist who rocked it through the MANY hours it took to shoot hundreds of photos and made sure everything was in the perfect place; David Green, aka Starvin-Artist, for his brilliant illustrations throughout the book; Dr. Heather Delaney, my amazing and talented proofreader; and last, but certainly not least, Fielden Willmott, my editor, who was a huge help in making this book come together.

I would also like to thank the supply houses and block makers that were big supporters of this project; Judith M Millinery, Jolie Femmes, Torb & Reiner, Guy Morse-Brown, and Moonlight Feathers.

Jenny Pfanenstiel, international award-winning couture milliner and owner of Formé Millinery, makes handmade hats for women, gentlemen, and children. Her one-of-a-kind hats are created using age old techniques that date back over 100 years, and include steaming and blocking over hat blocks, as a true couture milliner once did. In addition to incorporating traditional millinery skills, Jenny has mastered the art of hand manipulation of traditional and nontraditional millinery materials, creating "sculptures" for the head.

As a Milliner, she is known for her dedication to quality and using materials from France to Australia and incorporating these materials to truly make one-of-a-kind pieces. "As a couture milliner, my goal is to make a person feel sensational in my hats. I want them to look into the mirror and feel transformed, almost as if they are one with the creation of the hat." When a client comes into her hat shop for a custom hat, she provides an *experience*. She measures their head; they go through the different colors of straw or wool, and pick out the appropriate color. They talk about embellishments and what would work best. In a couple weeks' time, the customer has a handmade, one-of-a-kind hat made just for him or her.

Jenny has created hats for some of the world's most fashionable ladies, including Oprah Winfrey, First Lady Michelle Obama, Barbara Corcoran from the TV show *Shark Tank*, and actress Regina Taylor. Jenny also has created beautiful hats for productions with the Joffrey Ballet and the Goodman Theatre in Chicago. You can find her hat collections in specialty boutiques around the world, and in magazines such as, *Vogue*, *Tatler*, *Country Living*, *Vigore*, and *Belle Armoire*. She is also a featured milliner for the Kentucky Derby showcasing her race hats in various media outlets.

Jenny has also teamed up with McCall Patterns in creating flat pattern hats which are available through your local craft store and the McCall's website.

Millinery is a craft that Jenny wants to keep alive. She teaches couture millinery instruction around the world in group and private workshops, including basic blocking on wooden hat blocks, to sculptural hats using jinsin. She is currently working on opening the Formé School of Millinery, which will be the only year-round school within the United States dedicated to just millinery instruction. It will be a credited millinery school focusing on all aspects of hat-making which would include flat pattern hats, to specializing in a specific genre such as, derby, bridal, and theatrical hats.

Jenny Pfanenstiel
Couture Milliner/Hat Sculptor/Author/Educator/Owner
Formé Millinery Hat Shop
1860 Mellwood Ave. Suite #122-A
Louisville, KY 40206
www.formemillinery.com
formefashion@usa.net
(773) 719-7307
Making One-of-a-kind Hats, for One-of-a-kind People

Index